Ladies With Purpose And They Overcame

A Copulation of Women Life Experiences

Yolanda Y. Everett, BA., MA.

LADIES WITH PURPOSE: AND THEY OVERCAME

Table of Contents

SPECIAL THANKS & ACKNOWLEDGEMENTS

I would like to thank each and every one of these strong ladies who participated in this project; for your willingness to share your life with millions of other ladies.

I would like to also thank my mentor, my agent, my friend, my sister in the gospel, Apostle Alicia George for believing in me, and her faithfulness and spirit of excellence to see that this book comes to fruition.

Last, but surely not least, I would like to thank and acknowledge my handsome husband, my all-in-one, my biggest supporter, my ride-or-die, my loving soul mate for his insight, his encouragement, and his patience as I burn the midnight oil. I love you, Honey, with all of my heart, my soul, and my being. Thank you for believing in me and the vision that God has entrusted me with.

DEDICATION

This book is dedicated to all those ladies who did not think that they could make it...but did. And to all those ladies that feel as if they cannot make it...you will.

FOREWORD

Get ready to embark on a journey of life-filled experiences of challenges, difficulties, trials, and victories that women like you have overcome. This will be a time to reflect on what you may be facing at this time in your life, get inspiration, restoration, and even direction on how you will come through.

As you read and meditate on these experiences, you may even find yourself walking in each writer's shoes. Allow the Lord to even speak to the very "core" of what you are walking through at this time. You may even experience "healings" from past experiences that will navigate you to even greater freedom.

I have no doubt that you will grow to appreciate the courage of these women who have been transparent in telling their stories. Please know it is the hope of everyone who contributed to this publication that every reader would discover "nuggets of truths" that are specific to their own journey, be encouraged, strengthened, and even experience newfound freedoms in their own lives.

Open the book and begin your journey in "And They Overcame." Allow the Holy Spirit to speak to you. Position yourself for restoration and to overcome in your journey. God's plan for you is far above and beyond what you can imagine or think.

Thank you, Yolanda Everette Johnson, for your diligence in completing this book; and thank you for your dedication and commitment to the success of all women as well. I decree that everyone who reads "And They Overcame" and apply any principles that are conveyed by the infinite "Wisdom of and Guidance" of the Holy Spirit will yield a great harvest of fruit of "overcomers" in every field.

Professor Carol A. Williams

PREFACE

When the going gets tough, the tough gets going – maybe a cliché for some, but for a lot of women facing struggles daily, there's no option but to face them and move on. Listening to their struggles offers an insight into what they faced at every step in becoming the people they are now – a beacon of hope for others. We can mouth all the platitudes we want – *every cloud has a silver lining, there is light at the end of the tunnel,* etc. – but we can understand struggle only if we live through it and understand what the other person is going through. All of us face challenges, but how many of us don't give up but use those challenges to our advantage? Those who do, become an inspiration for all of us. Fortunately, the world has a lot of examples of such inspiring souls. Let's talk about women who not only fought all the odds and emerged as winners but also made the world a better place in their own way. "Heroes are people who have given their lives to something bigger than themselves." My heroes:

JoAnn Johnson
Maya Angelou
Mother Ora Nell Thomas
Mary Ross
Mother Sarah Williams
Pastor Teresa Lane

This is a little drop in the bucket out of a large ocean of names. I keep on adding the stories and women's names to the list. So, don't feel alone, there are many like you and they have survived the hardship you are going through now and have left a legacy of strength. If you ever feel weak in this challenged dominated society, just visit the pages in this book and read the short story of a strong woman. This will surely give you some boost to survive the struggle and know that one day you will definitely overcome all your pain and stress.

"There is nothing new. Many succeeded before, such as my heroes stated above. And surely you can too."

INTRODUCTION

I hope and pray that those of you who choose to read this book, look at your own inner struggles and see the strengths that you have and will continue to gain from them. My desire is that you take note of the constant struggles that I have engaged in during my life tenure, gain insight, be motivated, and realize that all struggles are not unto death. There is an inner strength that comes out of all the struggles you may endure during your own life. I can truly say I am a strong woman – a woman that does not look for or expect handouts, but a woman of strength and courage. One that is constantly in hot pursuit of all her goals and dreams.

I am hopeful that this book will motivate and encourage you, build you up, and strengthen you. It will reassure you and offer insight on life's struggles and that they are good tools for building your character.

Carrying years of painful baggage (weights) can give you strong triceps and biceps, I want to reach those who think that all life has to offer them are struggles and heartaches. I want to reach those who feel that they are on their last leg and barely making it. I want to reach the single mom who feels that she must steal and/or prostitutes herself to make a living and to supply her children with their needs. I want to reach the child who does not think that they can make it in life due to a broken home. I want to reach the dreamer who feels that his/her dreams are outlandish and unobtainable. I want to reach out to those that have open wounds and hurts from their past that they continue to struggle with and not let go of. I want to reach that optimistic person who knows and sees the light at the end of the tunnel but is getting wayward and faint at heart.

Yes, I found out the hard way. I found out that yes there is strength in the struggle. With so much pain and hardship; so much loneliness, so much agony; problems and troubles. With all this, the Lord says, "my grace is sufficient for thee, my daughter."

This book is a reflection of my life and how God Himself ministered to my soul, directly. This book is a reflects on the struggles within me and the love and concern, mercy, and grace that God has constantly shown me. Even when I felt all alone, with my back up against the wall, God gave me strength and power to look up to Him from which came all my help. I am reminded at this point, the poem "FOOTPRINTS." Those times when I felt at my lowest, this poem would come to mind. We look around and wonder where God is and if He knows that we are having some challenging times. We look about ourselves and see no evidence that God is with us. But, when we call upon Him, He is right there and saying, "my child I am carrying you through and that is why you only see one set of footprints."

Yes, I want to lift your spirit, stir up your inner man encourage your heart, and help you to realize that *THERE IS STRENGTH IN THE STRUGGLE*.

Always remember:

2 Corinthians 4:8-9 KJV:vs8 We are troubled on every side, yet not distressed; we are perplexed, but not in despair. vs9. Persecuted, but not forsaken; cast down, but not destroyed.

PASTOR YOLANDA Y. EVERETT:
THERE IS MORE TO ME THAN THE EYES SEE

IN THE BEGINNING

55 years old! Who would have thought that I would have survived to be 55 years old!?

I often heard my parents' conversation with others about my illnesses. My mother often joked that the doctors did not have to swat me on my bottom to get me to cry when I was born because I came out sneezing. From that day forward, I had allergies and sinusitis. And to top it all off, I was asthmatic until the age of 11.

My second home was the office of Dr. Robert Cureton and Morningside Hospital. At the age of five, I was diagnosed with ulcers and hence, there were many foods that I could not eat such as fried foods, hard foods, nuts, apples, and no acidic items. Due to allergies, I could not eat oranges or chocolate. My parents resorted back to feeding me baby food. Can you imagine a five-year-old kid eating baby food?

The worst part of my childhood was from kindergarten to fourth grade. I was always absent from school due to illness...if it was too hot or too cold. I couldn't go to school. If it was raining, I couldn't go to school. Thank God my parents knew the great physician, the Lord God Almighty!

TURNING POINT

My fifth-grade year was my first time with perfect attendance. That was a turning point in my life health-wise.

WHO AM I - IDENTITY CRISIS

I took a special interest in my sister, whom I deemed *simply gorgeous.* I watched her put makeup on and do her hair. She wore the most stylish clothes. I started thinking to myself, *that's who I want to be.* I started wearing her clothes. My sister was larger than I, but I would put on extra layers so that they would fit me tightly. When I was almost home, I would take everything off so that she or my mother wouldn't know.

Even still, I could not find my niche as to who I was supposed to be. I hung out with a girl named Lorna. We called her "Momma Lorna." She was the one who introduced me to smoking weed. We would go on the PE yard with several others, and they would light up. At that time, we were in Junior High School, I would watch them smoke but I was more of the lookout person. I did hit it a couple of times, but they always said, "Girl, you don't know what you're doing, give it back." I never knew what was meant by inhaling. I wanted to be cool, and I wanted to be accepted. I wanted an identity.

During my ninth-grade tenure, I had my share of issues and challenges: trying to "fit in where I could get in." There was another group of girls that I tried to hang out with from my neighborhood. We would walk to school together sometimes. They were more advanced than I, so I started to gravitate towards them. They, too, smoked cigarettes. Yes, ninth graders. I never smoked a cigarette, didn't like the smell; not to mention the smoke agitated my allergies. I would put one to my lips as if I was smoking. One day, Cynthia, one of the other girls burst my bubble by yelling out, "You don't even know what you're doing...it's not even lit." Yes, embarrassed.

I knew, at that point, they were not the group for me either.

I started walking to school with my cousin. Yes, I had another run-in with being the lookout. I wanted to be cool. I wanted to be accepted. One day, my cousin and I were walking on the sidewalk of the school, and I had a cigarette that I took from my sister's purse. It wasn't lit but I had it in my hand. Security saw me and I just knew that this would get me some "cool points." But no. The only point I got was suspension.

Remember, the subtopic of this chapter in my life is *Who Am I: An Identity Crisis*? Well, once again, I tried to get in where I fit in. I started dressing differently. Wearing clothes like my sister. Nice blouses and skirts. Boys started noticing me at this time and I started noticing them. *Oh yes*, I started noticing them!

I met Dwayne at this time, who was in high school and got out before we did. He would come up to the school to hang out with his cousin and started to walk me partially home. I said partially because my mom didn't allow me to have a boyfriend yet. Not even at 16 – my first date was at the age of 18.

Growing further and hanging out with Dwayne, I developed an interest in gangs, *or rather the gangsters*. It was unbeknown to me that he was a member of the Eight Tray Gangster Crips. I was accepted. I tried to fit in as best I could, but I stuck out like a sore thumb. I dressed and talked differently so needless to say the girls that were in the gang did not accept me, so I hung out with the guys. They treated me differently from the girls. They participated in various sexual encounters. Dwayne, who I will keep his nickname private, treated me well and showered me with jewelry. I would give it to my cousin to keep for me on a daily basis. He did not mind me being young and fresh. He never tried anything, so of course, his homies didn't. I knew that they were involved in sexual activities, including my man. But I didn't mind because that kept the heat off me. Just the idea of sex scared me to no end.

Another turning point in my young naive life was when I started seeing real OG gangsters hanging out at my school. I mean the older OGs! The real OGs.

I was not scared of them...Well, only one (he was four feet tall and had a loud voice). Everyone feared Crazy K. But they intrigued me. I knew so many gangsters from various gangs. I didn't know about rivalries and what was wrong with hanging out with people from different gangs. I found out though. As a matter of fact, one of the gangs, the Rolling 60's Crips, started calling me Lady Insane because they knew that I knew a lot of other gangs' affiliates. When one gang member found out that I knew other gang members from a rivalry sect, they came to my house and placed a comb by my mother's gas tank. He called that morning and told me to be careful and not be a traitor because they could blow up my family. He then told me to go look at my mom's car. I saw the comb and I knew who it belonged to.

That was close. Or at least I thought I was cleared. I found myself hanging out at the hub of one of the other gangs at a park and I heard motors racing and cars zooming. Everyone started running and yelling, "They're shooting...get down!" *Wow*, I was involved in a drive-by shooting! One of the guys was shot on the butt and another on the shoulder.

The hand of God was upon me at that time. I didn't get shot – nothing happened to me.

You know, I was not a promiscuous girl. I was a virgin up to the age of 18 but, oh my God, I saw these guys pull a train on my friend. In case you do not know what a "train" is – It is when guys all have sex with the same girl. They take turns. I was scared. To me, it was rape. I was sitting there on the sofa watching. Finally, one of them said, "You're a little girl, you don't even need to be here—get out of here."

I did just that!

On the way home I started thinking to myself and wondering if this is what it's all about. No, I didn't need to be there. It was at that time that realization set in, and I no longer hung out with gangs.

My life changed and my thoughts about sex did too. At that age, I had no clue about sex. Most girls were already active. Not me. I believe that experiencing the sight of a train being pulled on someone placed a damper on my mind about sex.

So, yes, I've had many challenges and differences in my life, especially not knowing who I am or for that fact not really knowing *whose* I am.

WHAT NEXT?

As time progressed, I still had difficulties with understanding my identity. I was placed in all advanced placement classes in my high school years. Okay, so that's one thing I did know and that is I was a smart...perhaps too smart for my own good.

I graduated with honors from Crenshaw High School and was accepted to several universities and it was decided for me to go to Cal State LA. Yes, my mother decided for me. This was the closest university. I was yet sheltered even going into my adulthood. My mom thought that the other schools were too far away from home. I guess she did not know the extra- curriculum activities that I found myself engaged in beforehand.

I majored in Psychology since I was interested in the mental psyche, especially with the mentality of criminals. I might've been a Criminologist, criminalistics, however, as luck would have it, I found myself yet again entangled in gangs.

On my way home from school one day, I was approached by a gentleman in a very nice Mercedes-Benz. Oh boy, it was nice, gold edition. The driver asked me if I wanted a ride and that he wanted to talk with me. I stopped and we talked for a moment. His name was Lee. I gave him my phone number... We talked for a couple of days. I didn't have any idea who this smooth cute guy was. I found out that he was a dope dealer of the notorious Benzo Family drug cartel.

The Benzo Boys was a high-level operative in the infamous Crenshaw Baldwin Hills area known for trafficking cocaine in major urban areas.

I was fine with that! After all, he was fine!

We became close friends. He liked the way I talked, often saying that I talked like a white girl or he would call me a "smart preacher's daughter."

As time went on, he would ask me to remember codes, calculations, and figures for him. He finally asked me to maintain his accounting ledger. I didn't know what I was doing but I agreed. I maintained drug deal transactions for him and eventually became the accountant for the Benzo Family Cartel.

I had no idea what I had gotten myself involved in. All I know is that I kept the numbers and when someone did not report all the proceeds and there was a discrepancy, it was up to me to report that to Benzo Lee and he would handle it...and yes, I mean, handle it!

Just imagine me, *Yolanda*, an accountant for the drug cartel. *Yes*, that was me. I did this for quite some time.

I was driven around in nice luxury cars. They respected me and treated me with dignity and honor because I ran the numbers. I was their prize possession.

This criminal activity that I found myself involved in at this time became lucrative for me and I found success in it by trafficking and hiding funds in bank accounts.

My book smarts and meek spirit helped me to rise to a top-level in the infamous Benzo Boys Family business.

Oh, what did I get myself involved in?

Ladies With Purpose

My time with the drug cartel abruptly stopped when Benzo Lee was picked up and charged for drug trafficking.

I was truly thankful for this breakthrough and that nothing happened to me nor my family. I was also thankful that the system worked. I never heard back anymore from The Benzo Family after Benzo Al cashed in on all the funds and went underground in hiding. I heard years later that Al was found murdered with his penis stuffed in his mouth.

PARTY CHURCH GIRL

During my tenure at CSULA, my girlfriends were all students and we partied, partied, partied.

Along with the partying, club hopping, church-going lifestyle, I began to look at life differently. I was getting tired of this duo life. I started wanting more from life. I attended church faithfully and taught young adult Sunday school class.

One day, my girlfriends were preparing to go out to the Florentine Gardens, and I did not want to go. I expressed this, one by one, as each girl called me. The next thing I know the girls were at my house. I got dressed and went.

I felt bad. I felt paranoid. I didn't want to be there. My demeanor for the night expressed this. I did not dance. I did not talk with the "ties" (this is what I called cute guys). Around 11 PM, I asked for the keys to Natalie's car so I could go sit in the car.

Oh God, help me. I don't want to live like this anymore. I want a good life. You said that if I confessed my sins, you would forgive me. You said that if I confessed with my mouth and believe in my heart that you were raised from the dead, I shall be saved. I believe Lord.

It was at this time that I accepted the Lord as my Savior on the floor of the backseat of Natalie's car.

I was saved in March 1985.

NEW LIFE

This was the beginning of a change in my life. I came to the realization that the Lord God Almighty had purpose and destiny in store for me. It is by God's grace and His unfeigned mercy and love that I am alive. I got past an illness, sickness, disease; I got past gang warfare and violence; I got past smoking; I got passed having guns pulled on me. All of that was for a reason. Jeremiah 29:11 KJV says, "God knows the plans He has towards me plans to do me good and not evil' plans to give me hope and a future."

The next few years, after getting saved and filled with the Holy Spirit, life changed.

I found a new Love in Christ Jesus. I began a new love life. I was faithful in church and did not look back.

Two years later, I was married with children.

THERE IS STRENGTH IN THE STRUGGLE

I laid in my bed with the feeling of loneliness and isolation. I felt imprisoned within my own self. No one to call, no one to talk with, no friends, no significant other, no one to pray with me. I turned over and began to sob uncontrollably. I grabbed the three small, lifeless-like bodies that lay on the side of me. My comfort and strength: my three babies, Daniel, Allen, and April. *Oh, God,* I thought to myself, *life is so hard. In life, there is so much hatred, so much pain, so much trouble, so many struggles just to survive. Oh, God, help me to be a good mom, a better mom. Help me to raise my three little bundles of blessings in the fear and admonishment of You. I am so alone. Life is so hard. I cannot seem to see my way through. I do not have anyone to turn to; no one to hold me during these times of distress; no one to whisper those sweet words of comfort, "I love you. It is going to be alright." I don't know which way to go.* I held them tighter against my breast. The last thing that I remembered murmuring to myself is, *there is strength in the struggle.*

Failed marriages. I do not have my three bundles of blessings to hold and to love on. But I have my sanity and my sense of will to live a life of purity and happiness, a life full of joy and yes strength...I found myself once again, wondering and rehearsing those same words as I did in 1993. *Life is so hard. I cannot seem to see my way through. I do not have anyone to turn to; no one to hold me during these times of distress; no one to whisper those sweet words of comfort, "I love you, and it is going to be alright." I don't know which way to go.* And finally, my life quote came to mind, *"there is strength in the struggle."*

When I think of women of strength, I think of my mother, *JoAnn Johnson*, and my godmother, *Ora Nell Thomas*, as well as *Pastor Teresa Lane*, and of course, *myself*.

Where did the strength of these fore mothers come from? Born during times of racism and poverty, when girls/women were seen and not heard – worked at doing all the household chores and taking care of five, six, ten children, washing, ironing, even while little Johnny was on her hip. Today, we have emerged, and this is a profession that we now call *Domestic Engineers*.

Where did their strength come from? Was there an external force or an internal power? Nevertheless, with all the drama that went on in their lives, there was a sense of strength that kept a smile on their faces – their inner strength was the glue that kept the family afloat and husbands coming home day after day to a home filled with love, nurture, and wholesomeness.

Have you ever felt like just walking away? Walking away from everybody and everything? Not packing, just put shoes on, any old shoes, and just walk away into eternal nothingness? Your career, your family, your ministry? Including walking or attempting to even walk away from your own self? Have you ever asked the question *why I am here and what is my purpose?* Today, this seems like a cliché in church.

Have you ever asked the question *why am I experiencing such hardship, such pain, and so many struggles?* What about this, this is a good one: *God, do You hear me, do You love me, and if so, why don't You answer me, I don't hear You?*

Because of the mayhem and mishaps of life, do you often feel dismayed, discouraged, downtrodden, and tired? Well, join the club in which I am your humble President. I often wondered if things would really work out for me. I know the scripture in **Roman 8:28** that says, **"All things work together for the good of those that love God and to them that are the called according to His purpose."** I often thought, *when will the working out for me start working together for my good?*

I began to always question God: *God, you can't possibly use me, an undone, wretched person that I am. God, are you sure that you saved me and called me? Me? Are you sure?* I could hardly hear that faint answer, "yes, I called you, my daughter."

If any of these questions have found a place in your mind, it's alright and this book is for you, including myself, who has faced such struggles in life. If truth be told, at some time or other, I am sure that even the most supreme prophetic televangelist – the most high of the most high – has faced such trying times as well.

Sometimes, or at least most of the time, the struggle is within our own self. This is the most severe tug of war. I struggled at times wondering *who* I am, *what* I am, *whose* I am. I wonder at times if I was really called into the ministry. I struggled with this not only because of the inner tug of war that was going on within, but the outward struggle between myself and life. The struggle from outside forces was not so hard itself, but the inner struggle, the low self-esteem and conquering, that was what gave me the momentum to go on, to pursue my divine purpose and destiny, who I was created to be and whom I belonged to.

I thought for sure, by now I would be further along down the pathway of success...spiritual success that is. This is what is important to me. Not the fine cars, not the big homes, nor the fancy suits and shoes. But to do the will of God, my Father in ministry.

I struggled with myself. I struggled with low self-esteem. I even struggled with God. Yes, even with my Heavenly Father, and I struggle with man. *Man!?* Interestingly enough, man has always dictated to me who and what I am to be. *Yolanda, you are sick. Yolanda, you are controlling. Yolanda, you are rebellious. Yolanda, you are headstrong. Yolanda, Yolanda, Yolanda...*But, no one ever said, "Yolanda, the Lord says... (you fill in the blanks with positive reinforcements)." Thanks be to God, who sends His Rama word and said, "Daughter, only say who I say you are and don't accept anything else. Don't even let it enter into your ear-gate. Rebuke, reject, and don't accept what others say that is not in accordance with what I say, only what I have told you that you are – that is what and who you are."

Yes, the struggle without is almost as harsh as the struggle within. But, this struggle, this entanglement with forces beyond my control, yields to the inner man and cause friction, doubt, and unbelief. This leads to the tug of war between who God says I am and who man says I am, and ultimately who I perceive myself as being.

Whoever thought that life would be so hard, whoever thought that the cares of this world would lead to the thought of suicidal tendencies dancing and prancing about my mind? Yes, who would have thought that the struggles of life would cause so much grief, so much misery, and so much pain, so much discomfort, so much...STRENGTH.

You may wonder why I say that struggles cause one to be strong...because it does. I learned this the hard way, kicking and screaming. I can only imagine times in life with no struggles. That will not happen, let me tell you. Life, itself, is a challenge within its own right. You can allow these struggles to break you and defeat you or you can allow them to build you up and make you strong. One of my brothers used to say that "challenges make you strong and put hair on your chest." I would prefer to say, "when life deals you lemons, make lemonade."

Life still had a lot of struggles in store for me. I married against the wishes of fellow church leaders

There are things that can trip you up and dampen your spirit, "the first thing is failure – or even the fear of failure."

But an important part of achieving what we have set out to do – and something that seems to be particularly difficult for us women – is overcoming bumps in the road along the way. We forget that failure is often a necessary part of eventual success. To remind ourselves of this, I have gathered the stories of fearless women who experienced hardships as myself before ultimately becoming legends in our perspective fields.

EMOTIONAL ABUSE: THE INVISIBLE TRAIN WRECK

In hindsight, I never felt my relationships with my previous husbands were abusive. One would certainly think it would be easily detected – easily felt. I never believed it could have been part of my life. The abuse crept into my life effortlessly and I subconsciously learned to survive through the horrific emotional and spiritual dysfunction. I despised it yet lived through it.

Unlike physical abuse, emotional and spiritual abuse is often more difficult to recover from, as the scars are more self-destructive. There are no visible marks, and friends and family can barely detect your pain.

In the beginning of my first "mock marriage," I thought my relationship struggles were the typical marital woes everyone faced as newlyweds. I felt determined to work through the battles I constantly faced. I thought it was that part of my marital journey where I would suffer through and learn to accept my significant other's faults. I was proud of my ability to survive. The scars on my heart began to thicken and block my ability to love this human. Our dysfunctional relationship felt so wrong, but my learned ability to forgive trumped all my instinctive feelings.

I only had pride in caring for my babies.

The times I wanted to leave were immeasurable. He was an expert at convincing me I would never see my oldest baby and that the kids would be split and would hate me forever. Self-doubt was inevitable. The abuse became such a profound part of my life, yet I stayed. The level of toxicity increased. I became very saddened during our last year together. At one low point, I developed introverted habits and found a hiding place in caring for my children. I felt trapped and unable to see how diminished my self-respect had become. I lost my ability to be combative in arguments because I'd rather keep the peace than trigger an emotional outburst.

The joy and happiness in my life was trapped underneath the misery. I worried more about my children's lives more than my own well-being. It became my normal. Truthfully, I did not even know what emotional and financial abuse was, or that it was considered domestic violence until I finally broke down and went into a secret spiritual warzone for guidance and direction. I began to fast and pray and cry out to God and was even more faithful to ministry and church and studying. Knowledge became a power for me. I began to research and read up on the issues I faced. They all resonated with me. I learned the best way to handle an abuser and how to leave an unhealthy marriage. So, I started banking all income and saving instead of paying bills.

This particular ex-spouse's goal was to gain control and power over me through all the belittling, financial control, and spiritual manipulation. His behavior had become unpredictable and troublesome. He made every attempt to use the word of God as a disciplinary weapon against me. The more I pulled away from his grip on me, the tighter he held on. I had to carefully plan my escape. The last few months we were together, I had to act like I would try to work on our relationship. I pretended to care, when deep down I hated him

I began regularly and faithfully to lay before God, which gave me instant perspective and strength. Every time I left my war room, I felt more powerful. My doubts and fears slowly dissipate. It was as if when I was inside the confines of his delusional world. I couldn't think straight or function as the strong woman I once was. His constant barrage of hurtful words kept me fenced in on the emotional merry-go-round. This vicious and toxic cycle was what we needed in each other as partners. He needed to be in control of my life, and I became accustomed to forgiving his bad behavior.

It took me an excruciating year of facing my fears to realize I had to leave, or I would never make it out. The strong fist of domestic violence would end up costing me my livelihood, which was that of my children. It wasn't up to me to help him see his evil ways or making him better. That was his karma. He had to help himself, and I knew I had to jump off the merry-go-round, no matter how difficult it would be.

I blindsided him and left while he was away one day. With the support of family, I started a new life. It was the scariest decision I had ever made, but I now consider it to be an exciting new beginning for me. A new chapter has begun. I now write my own future and that is the power of self.

Emotional and spiritual abuse is real and is as destructive to a human being as physical abuse.

If the abuser refuses to exit, you must have the will to walk out of the door. Make a plan, find a place – even if temporary. It's just material items. Your sanity is far more important than any replaceable structure.

Do research information about emotional abuse. Call women's centers in your area for free counseling and support. Knowledge is power. They can even help you with housing, finding free attorneys, and filing a Temporary Protection Order (TPO) if your situation warrants that. Mine did not!

Do not engage in any conversations with the abuser, especially after you leave. It's their tool for getting you back on that detrimental ride of abuse. My boundaries were not strong enough to guard off the hurtful words I wanted to leave behind. It must be an abrupt cut off from all communication. If you have kids, the abuser can communicate through attorneys.

Learn how to love yourself. **I DID!** Involve yourself in a great support group or ministry. **I DID!** Most importantly, don't look back. **I DIDN'T!**

Today, I thank God for His bountiful blessings, His faithfulness, and love for me. Yes, it's a new season. It is a new day. You must feel it within yourself, as I had to, the fresh aroma of the morning dew as it falls gently on the petals of each beautiful rose. Yes, I am finally strong enough, ready for the challenge of life's struggles that this day is bound to bring.

FROM BROKENNESS TO WHOLENESS

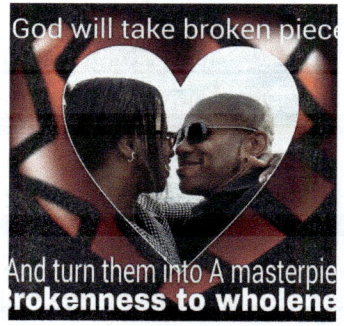

I am now married, and I thought to myself, *oh my God, he really called in challenges, spiritual warfare, emotional, and verbal, and spiritual abuse. Dysfunctional Lizum, discord, division, pride — these things are not to be in America; these are broken pieces.*

If truth be told, these are signs of immaturity and Laura got my switcher into perfect unity, perfect love cast out all fears, perfect trust in other words covenant marriage, and now I have a marriage that is ordained by God. I have a husband that loves me, and I love him; we were together in unity and in the spirit of love. Thank God for taking these broken pieces and turning them into His masterpiece.

I am healed and made whole.

God will take your broken pieces as well and turn them into His
masterpiece!
The supernatural has already begun.
In my marriage in my home
In the lineage, my children, and my children's children.
New people. New partnerships. New businesses...
More books are coming forth
Watch me as I soar in the name of Jesus!
Love even much more!

KATRINA LYLES:
DEPRESSION HAS FANGS...BUT I HAVE A SWORD

My life has certainly had its share of challenges, I think our greatest challenge is overcoming the thoughts that come to bring us doubt and pain. I'm grateful to say that throughout all my life, my most challenging moments have always seen the face of grace. I simply remember from a young child, the feeling of not being seen. I felt that I wasn't liked or heard enough, though I had everything around me that proved differently. I battled with these thoughts until I understood that I had the power to speak to them.

I've learned through growth and experience that whatever you believe, it is so and with that realization, I had to practice readjusting my thoughts and renewing my mind daily. I trust that God created me to be wonderful and no weapon shall prosper against my life. I see doubt and negativity like weapons that come in vulnerable times of our lives.

Yes, and because I see their tactics, I have the tools to keep them at bay; I will not allow even my own thoughts to upset the plan that God has for me. I hope that every woman who reads this knows that with awareness, reflection, and daily practice we can heal our wounds and grow to walk in the authentic power that God has given each of us.

Depression is reversible, think of it like any other disease; a build-up of mucus, except depression is like fungi. Depression grows on us. It molds upon us and decays our spirits. Depression is a sunken feeling.

I remember being a teenager and facing depression, it hit me, it teased me, it pushed me around and tried to hold me; depression was my bully. At the time I was facing it daily, I felt it at the pit of my belly on weekends, I was in hell. Throughout the week, school kept me functional and distracted from the pain but every time I came home and looked in the mirror, I could not face my own reflection. I was not enough, my hair wasn't long enough, my face wasn't pretty enough, I did not feel smart enough, fun enough or loved enough.

During this time of my life, I ached for God to see me. I cried out many times believing that I was forgotten; I imagine that's what our ancestors felt like during the slave trade – that God had forgotten about them, aching, sick, defeated, and depressed. No one understands the turmoil and bondage of depression until they have faced its fangs and how it pressures into your life, gripping you with the force of a striking snake. Depression is unhealed pain knocking at your door as if to say, "It's our anniversary!"

I want no part of your trauma depression. Hold on to your drama – I pray you away with the power of rebuke from my momma. You cannot have my soul.

My purpose is to live life wholly, and though you may come, I declare you cannot hold. You will not bound me in spirit or keep me from life. I sacrificed my tears to swim a Nile River from you. I learned a way called Victory that taught me to speak over my day and talk to God anyway. I let go of my fears and shared my secrets; revealed some truths I thought I'd never say and cried in the arms of God's protection.

This took a turn and set my soul on fire. I was redeemed, saved from the pit of hell. God brought me out of a dark place where the pain of my forefathers had me bound. I am healed, rather set free; the healing is a process throughout life, but I'm no longer bound by the pain.

I am actively healing every day from the bruises on this tender soul and God is my redeemer. Truth set me free, fearlessness set me free; by my words and the sound of my voice God heard my cry and set me free. I am no longer chained or bound in sin because God made a way of escape; picked me up out of hell and placed me on solid ground. God filled my cup so that I could help heal the world.

Many of us know the fangs of depression, it strikes then strikes again, and at each return, it grips more deeply. When depression returns, the timing is not up to you but the choice to live or die is always yours. Choose to live and pick up your sword and walk.

DR. DARLENE JOY BRYANT:
A LIFE STORY IN A SNAPSHOT

The journey began March 2, 1978, in San Francisco, California. I had two wonderful parents who had barely graduated high school, but had been in love since they were 13 years old. Two years later, my sister, Elisha, came along but through that, sickness was discovered. My mother, Veronica, slipped into a coma after my sister was born. The next year she passed out at work and her co-worker got her to the hospital before tragedy struck because her kidneys had failed. The culprit was lupus. My father, Les, worked very hard at a grocery store and eventually became our only source of income due to my mother having to go on disability. My mother taught us how to cook at an early age because she had to attend dialysis treatments several times a week. Elisha and I were "latch key kids," wearing the house key on a shoestring around my neck, back when it was relatively safer for children to walk home by themselves from elementary school. My parents gave us a wonderful life, despite how the circumstances dealt with them. We never understood the sacrifices they made until we were older.

I fell in love at age 18 and left home at 19 to move in with my grandmother in Sacramento. I didn't want to have to follow my parent's rules. I was a straight-A student but missed scholarship opportunities to go to my dream school, Xavier University of Louisiana. I was too busy chasing after that boy. I ended up going to

31

Ladies With Purpose

Community College instead, which was fine with me because I could be with him. I got pregnant with my son, Corde, at 19 and planned on marrying his father. When my son was one year old, I realized that his father was not going to mature from smoking marijuana while I was at work and school, and that relationship ended. In comes the knight in shining armor. I met the man whom I would marry and eventually divorce in college. He was such a Godly young man, and he taught me a lot about the word of God. My mother loved him and I'm so happy she was able to meet him before she passed away from heart complications due to the Lupus. I went through a complete period of depression at her loss when she was only 40 and I was 22. The knight in shining armor helped me get through that as well with the help of my amazing father and sister. We got married when I was 23 and he was only 20. We were heavily involved in our church, and we had a beautiful baby girl, Aryeal. However, he, unfortunately, turned from what he knew was right and began to indulge in infidelity. The last situation resulted in the woman getting pregnant. I was willing to stay and work it out, but he wasn't. He moved out to live with her, and I was a single mother again.

One would think that with all the time I spent talking to the Lord, I would have made better decisions. Well, I didn't. I fell in love with a married man, who was also a Deacon at my church, who was also married to someone I had been good friends with. He had pursued me for a long time, and when I tried to tell his wife and the Pastors about it, they didn't believe me. I was accused of seeking attention because my marriage had failed. So, when my husband left, I felt like I had nothing to lose and gave in. I am not making excuses for my reprehensible actions, but at 26, my judgment was horrible. He was older, had money, and was helping me out when my husband would not, and his marriage was experiencing difficulties. It seemed like a good deal. We spent a lot of time together, and we had been intimate twice during the relationship. We got caught when the assistant pastor saw me sneaking out the back door of his restaurant. I was ostracized from the church once everyone found out. However, I did still have a few friends left in the church who didn't pass judgment and forgave me for my part in it, one being Pastor Yolanda Everett. I did ask the Deacon's wife for forgiveness, and she told me that God would give her the strength to forgive. I pray that she has. I have finally forgiven myself.

I became a biology teacher in 2008, and my first job was at Garfield High School. I met a custodian named Tony, (aka A-Tone, aka Anthony) and we became very good friends, confidants, even. We were both going through a divorce. I had been separated from my ex for three years, but his was recent. The friendship turned into a joint rescue, where we realized we were both deserving of truly being loved. We got married in 2011, joining together a family of five kids. I became a mother to Zoe, Chloe, and Joey, in addition to Aryeal and Corde.

A-Tone was ordained as a Pastor in 2012, and I was ordained as a Pastor in 2017. We were both ordained as Apostles in 2017. I have a bachelor's degree in Biology, a master's degree in Secondary Education, and a Doctor of Educational Leadership and Management. My husband and I both also hold Doctorate of Divinity. We are the founding Pastors of The Family Center of Love, a growing church in Los Angeles, California. Corde (now 22) has recently finished his senior year at Morehouse College and is awaiting graduation after the current pandemic has eased, Zoe (20) will be entering into her junior year at Howard University this fall, and Aryeal (17) will be a freshman at UCLA this fall. Chloe (14) and Joey (11) will follow soon.

I am now the First Lady and Pastor of Educational Arts of the Family Center of Love, where my loving husband, Anthony "A-Tone" Bryant, serves as Senior Pastor. I received my calling to the Apostolic alongside my husband in 2017. I am the mother of five children, Corde (22), Zoe (19), Aryeal (17), Chloe (14), and Anthony (11). I first accepted my calling to ministry in 2009, when the Lord placed upon my heart to begin Purpose and Destiny Prayer Ministry. Purpose and Destiny operates under 1 Thessalonians 16-18: "Rejoice always, pray without ceasing, give thanks in all circumstances; for this is the will of God in Christ Jesus for you." This prayer ministry works hard to intercede on behalf of those who seek prayer, and myself and my team of prayer warriors enjoy standing in agreement with others in prayer. I am an enthusiastic praise and worship leader and I sing alongside my husband in many local events.

I work for the Los Angeles Unified School District, teaching high school Biology and whichever life science courses I am needed for. I received my Doctorate in Educational Leadership and Management from Capella University. I also received an Honorary Doctorate in Divinity from St. Thomas Christian University. I am excited about growing in the Lord, as well as growing as a wife, mother, daughter, friend, and sister day by day. I appreciate the wonderful life God has blessed me with and I wouldn't change my journey because any minor change would have impacted His plan for me.

SHELIA MARIE HALE:
MOTHER

orn April 12, 1952, to Chris and Mary Tyler. I grew up in Los Angeles California surrounded by daddy, mama, grandparents, aunts, uncles, and cousins. My father died when I was 12 years old. With the help of family, my mom, and the grace of God, I grew up.

I attended McCoy Memorial Baptist Church and Truly Missionary Baptist Church in Los Angeles. I attended 75th St. Elementary School, Brett Hart Junior High School, and John C. Fremont Senior High School.

I married my first husband on September 12, 1970, because of being pregnant. You see, back then as a Christian girl, if you got pregnant you either got married or find a way to give birth to your child and place that child up for adoption at least in some household or families.

My marriage lasted five years and I left because he was abusive and a cheater. I became a single parent having to deal with the threats of taking my child. I was not bringing him home when he should've been home – that was the way of trying to get me back when I finally decided to leave him. I never had to get a babysitter because my family members always stepped in to assist.

I never looked back but did have to explain to my son that it was not his fault that daddy and I were not together, and we couldn't live together, but we both loved him.

I worked in the insurance field as a file clerk and underwriter's associate. Thanks to Helser Insurance Company, I became acquainted with computers and met my husband. The first meeting of my husband and I was quite a great show. Not to mention my first encounter with computers

We married December 22, 1978, in Las Vegas. We had our firstborn on December 24, 1979. She experienced her first earthquake on January 1, 1980, and my family decided to name her Quackie. We lived in Los Angeles, having two more children a boy and a girl, and finally moved to Paris, California on August 2, 1985. After moving to Paris, I found my church New Hope Missionary Baptist Church of Riverside, California. I also found a job as a cashier at the corner store. I was fired after two years because a so-called trusted friend of the store owner lied on me.

I worked for Val Verde School District, not yet unified then as a seasoned worker but found a job as a certified nurse assistant where you are trained. I took a class at Sun City Confidence, where I found my trust and love as a caregiver. I became a caregiver for developmentally disabled (mentally and physically) adults.

Now, in between all of that, there had been some "church hurts." Chillwave Family Church is where my cousin was Pastor. The way that I was removed from playing the organ in my learning stage is tacky and hurtful in front of the entire congregation. I went back to my childhood church, McCoy Church, and a lot of families there and singing in the choir worked with the youth until I moved to Paris. I left New Hope Church, hurt, but this time, it was under God's divine hand He always has the last word and guides me in when to move and when to speak.

I was sent to Noon Sentry Baptist Church in Riverside California to begin my group. We married there until 2010, it was led by the Holy Spirit to return to my present church home, New Hope Missionary Baptist Church. It was here that my growth was able to flourish under our Pastor, in women's ministry leadership as well as to all the women of the Valley District and the California State Baptist Association.

I've been choir director teacher of youth and young adults for awesome children, whom I am very proud of and who they have become. It's been through God's grace and mercy that I am here. I am a uterine cancer survivor. My sisters of New Hope in Jake and the state of California were all there to support. Yes, I had my moments, but I didn't give up. I now know my assignment, under the function of the Holy Spirit, which is to pray for others.

I haven't stopped praying for all others yet. At the store, parking lot, on the phone, Facebook, wherever and whenever. I am your servant and here to see you. With this bout with cancer, my life is not over yet and so I will do everything in my power to do what God called me to do.

LADY KIMMY BLOUNT:
SHE MADE IT

Strength and honor are her clothing; and she shall rejoice in time to come.
Proverbs 31:25 KJV

THE STRUGGLE OF KNOWING HOW THINGS WOULD END

When I said, "I do," I never would have thought the marriage would end. Three years of something I thought was real was just a learning experience that brought me heartache, pain, and tears. I felt like giving up. Time after time I walked away broken, feeling like a failure.

But the truth is that all it did was make me a better me in the end. Years went by not knowing my self-worth. As time went by, I found my victory in Jesus Christ. You see, He restored every part of me. My heart went to true healing the moment I allowed God to work on me.

I am a better me today. I stand before you free and an overcomer. I am beautiful, smart, and an amazing woman because my father made me. Through my struggles came the birth of several books: *Learning to Love Yourself* and *What Doesn't Kill You, Makes You Stronger.*

I was united in Holy Matrimony with my husband and together we have five amazing children. I never thought that I would allow myself to love again. God knew just what I needed.

I have been performing throughout Southern California and have worked with EOGM Productions, Pid Production, GNA Universal Media, and much more. I have also worked with location production companies, such as Breaking Loose Productions, New Heights Ministries, and opening for the Hyphy 4 Christ, Inc. On Sunday, May 12, 2019, I became the visionary of Anointed One Ministries, Bloom Ministries (Being Lifted Out of Mess), Bloom Kidz, and Bloom Studios. Anointed One Ministries is based on **Joel 2:28-29 KJV: And it shall come to pass afterward, that I will pour out my spirit on all flesh; your sons and daughters shall prophesy, your old men shall dream dreams, your young men shall see visions; and also, on my servants and on my maidservants, I will pour out my Spirit in those days.**

My vision and mission is to help uplift others and guide them through whatever they may be facing and to lift people out of the mess they are in so that they too, can bloom into who they are to be. I did and I am thankful to God. I have learned the importance of praising and worshipping God and want to share my life lessons on such and how important it is for your everyday life. Another vital lesson that I learned, and I pray that you will gain this knowledge as well, and that is that we should show love, have faith, and be obedient.

Kimberly L. Blount remember the name!

This woman that you see has grown up to be who God created her to be. The things that she went through some self-hurt. You see she's not who she used to be. This next chapter has already begun. She didn't die in the process it just made us stronger.

#WhatsDoesntKillYouMakesYouStronger #DontDieInTheProcess #NewMe #HappyandFree #LevelUp #It'sAboutToGetReal #LetsGo

BLOOM

I am beautiful in my own right
I am unique and awesome inside and out
I am free from all the things that had me bound
No longer will I allow my past to haunt me
No longer will I allow what was or is said to dictate who I am to be
I have purpose and it lives right inside of me
I speak life over me and my family
We will make it
I will endure to the end
I will win
Today is a new day
I will live again
I am free from the hand of the enemy
Satan you cannot have me
I am loved and my mind is at peace
My heart is healed because Jesus, you died for me
So, no matter what yesterday tried to give me
I will accept who I am today
You see, this is me and I love me
Today, I let go of everything that hurt me
Being lifted out of mess so I can bloom into who God wants me to be.

MONIQUE HESTER:
I TRUST GOD

I would love to be an inspiration to you with a story based on actual events. God allowed two situations to take place in my life that caused me to step out of my comfort zone, and totally trust in Him. I am the mother of ten children, eight are still living at home. Life seemed to be going okay. I was in the process of working on mine and my husband's credit scores in hopes to buy a home by the end of 2019.

I had totally taken my eyes off God in that sense. I was a firm believer that I had to make this happen on my own and had convinced myself that, no prayers in the world would cause me to be able to become a homeowner unless I did certain steps on my own. But all of this soon changed by one phone call.

It was June 4th on a Tuesday in 2019 around 5p.m., I received a phone call while at work, from the manager of the apartments that we were renting. I had lived there for six years. The voice on the other end said, "Mrs. Hester, we received your rent, but it is being rejected, you need to try and get your money back so that you can move. We have decided not to renew your lease." You can only imagine the shock that I was in. She further told me that I needed to move out by the next day. When I asked her why, she said you know the whole robbery thing and you're buzzing in a car that ended up robbing a couple. I told her again, that I had no idea that it was someone that I didn't know that was buzzed in, that my children were out at church, and I thought that it was our church van ringing to be let in as usual. Anyway, they didn't believe me but thought that one of my sons had told some guys to ring our apartment so that they can come in and rob a couple. Of course, as God is my witness, none of this was true in any form. My son was totally innocent of their claims.

I hung up the phone with tears in my eyes and asked God to direct me that I needed a miracle. I called my husband and filled him in. I called the manager back and told her that I needed more time, that I could not move in one day. I let her know that I'd be off that Thursday and Friday and would be able to clean the apartment up and move by then. She agreed to our moving out by that Friday 5p.m. The next day, I began looking for apartments for rent, plus I was able to go online to my bank account and move the rent out of my account since it hadn't been posted yet. I found an apartment the next day, we had to stay in a hotel for a week until everything went through, regarding credit, employment, and rental checks. Fortunately, I owed the previous place no money, so they filled out the form in our favor, not mentioning those alleged untruths. I could see favor from God working. The woman charged me 279.00 for rent due for June 1st-5th. I paid her and never looked back.

We moved into the new apartment on June 11th, 2019. This was a very luxurious high-end apartment with four swimming pools and several upscale amenities. The apartment had a fireplace, two balconies, and was surrounded by trees, and huge mansions. I felt very proud to have been approved to live there. After moving in, I got comfortable with our living situation and was no longer looking for or desiring to buy a house at that time. I told myself one day when my credit scores reached the 700's I'll start seriously looking at homes. My credit scores were 666, 654, and 664. I was just grateful to be in this expensive place. The rent was $1620 a month plus you had a separate amenity bill, water, trash, and other fees. Every month I was paying well over $1800 a month. But I was still just happy and contented to be in such a nice quiet beautiful area. God will always give you double for your trouble. The previous apartment complex sent me a total of over $700.00 back. Our security deposit was only $50.00 Go figure.

I decorated the new apartment with photos everywhere and made the place nice and homey. Well, my excitement and contentment were short-lived.

I received a phone call on Tuesday November 26th, 2019, on my job from one of my sons, telling me that one of my 15-year-old twin boys had been handcuffed and placed in the back of the police car. I was told that he was being accused of throwing rocks at windows where people lived and breaking them. I spoke to the policeman over the phone and told him that my son has autism and that this is totally out of character for him. He is usually very well-mannered and shy, and that I would pay for the damages done. I begged the policeman to please let my son go back home with his brother. He did. According to my son that called me, he stated that the neighbors whose windows were broken said that they weren't pressing any charges but that they just wanted it to stop.

Once home, I spoke to my son, and I asked him why he threw rocks at the neighbors' windows. He said, "I have no idea, Mommy, nobody lives there anyway, its dark inside." I told him that just because it's very dark back there didn't give him the right to bust windows and that people did live back there. It was strange because deep down inside I wasn't mad at him at all, I couldn't get upset like I wanted too. When my husband came home from work, I told him all the happenings and, like myself, he too found it very difficult to become upset. We both prayed that we would only have to pay for damages, and not be asked to move. This was our biggest fear, especially mine.

The next morning, November 27th, the apartment manager knocked on our front door with the security guard. She basically said that the damages are a lot and that it's in cooperates hands now, that she will let us know what the next steps will be. Once she spoke those words, I had the deepest most sunken feeling in my stomach like never before. She left our apartment with the words spoken, for us to try and have a wonderful Thanksgiving.

After she left. I began preparing our Thanksgiving dinner. I cooked a meal fit for a king, all along praying inside that all we have to do is pay for broken windows. I pushed everything from my mind, and we all enjoyed a wonderful Thanksgiving, filled with laughter, food, and family games. My eldest daughter and her family came by, and my daughter who's in college was over that week.

On November 29th, 2019, Good Friday, I opened the front door around 4p.m. to find a notice taped to our door that read, Attention to my husband's name and all occupants, YOUR LEASE IS BEING TERMINATED AND YOU MUST MOVE OUT ON OR BEFORE DECEMBER 1ST, FOR A NONE RENT VIOLATION. Failure to do so by the said date will result in your being sued and evicted before a Justice of the Peace.

I sat down on the couch in my living room totally speechless. My fears had come true. I didn't know what to do, or how to wrap my mind around what was happening. My daughter later told me that I said, how can God bless this mess? What are we going to do now? I remember feeling like I was cursed or something, to be asked to move from two different residences in one year, six months apart. Surely, God was nowhere in this. I was distraught and began to do some quick thinking. We rented a U-Haul truck and packed up our whole apartment, we cleaned the apartment from top to bottom, washed walls, cleaned bathrooms etc... I was determined to leave a good impression, and for them to see the kind of people that we really are.

On Sunday, December 1st, 2019, we moved into a two-room hotel in the area, paying $738.00 a week for like three weeks, until I asked about a better rate. We then started paying $686.00 a week. We continued to drop our four high school students off at the same bus stop for school. I was determined to keep some sort of normalcy for them. On Monday, December 2nd, on my way to work, I cried and prayed to God for a direction. I was determined not to ever pay rent again. As I drove to work the song by Britt Nicole was playing that is titled "Walk on the Water." It's amazing because I had heard this song many times, but for the first time, I actually heard the words loud and clear, let your faith fall to the ground, and about stepping into the unknown. Your faith is all it takes, and you can walk on the water too.

Two weeks later on Sunday, December 15th after church, Lawrence and I went to an open house, we were the only ones to show up. During the tour, we discovered that the house had flooded in Hurricane Harvey. This was discouraging news, so we were in a decision to either accept the discovered information or pass on this house. As we were driving back towards the freeway, we passed up a huge corner lot home sitting on my right side, that had a for sale sign in the front yard. I quickly told Lawrence to turn around so that I could write the number down and call the agent to inquire. After writing down the phone number, I had a doubting feeling come over me. The thoughts flooded my mind that I could never be able to buy such a huge and beautiful house. What if my credit isn't good enough yet, etc....? I had been checking my credit daily and working on our credit scores for almost two years.

My plan was to wait until my scores were at least 700 plus to even think about buying. I had to push all of my fears and doubts away and keep pressing toward my goal. Later that day, I went to work, where the realtor from the open house we had decided to pass on, called, and said that he has a loan officer that can work with us to help us get into a home by Christmas. The loan officer, Cassandra, called me, and we started the process of giving all of our info to her so that she could pull our credit scores. After she called me back, my second worst fear became a reality. My Fico Mortgage middle score was low at 613. My husband's middle Fico Mortgage score was 697. I was told that by law they have to use the spouse with the lowest score. This news was very daunting for me. However, she did say that our debt to ratio income was very good and that we both had a solid employment history. And that we had no late payments, and our credit card usage was low. I had two negatives on my report that they only counted 120.00 against us. So, we agreed to go ahead and move forward with buying a house, she assured me that she would do her best to give us as good a rate as possible and to get us prequalified. This is when I let her know that we were not interested in the house we saw at the open house and asked her if she could send us more homes to look at. She let us know that she would tell the realtor that showed us the house, and that he can send us a list of homes in that price range to view. I received his list of houses but did not like any of them, so I told him that I would be gathering a list together of homes that we would like to view, he agreed.

I looked online on Monday, December 16th at Zillow.com, as I began to scroll down the page at all of the houses for sale, I spotted a huge corner lot home with a pool. The closer I looked at the house, the more I realized that this was the house that I wrote the number down too. I put that house at the top of the list and added four other houses. We viewed all of the houses on December 22nd, 2019. The huge house on the corner that we viewed first was the most beautiful house I had ever seen, both inside and out.

That night we made an offer on the house. Two days later the realtor called us and told me that our offer had been accepted. God really showed up and showed out. He opened up all kinds of doors for us. I was able to pay my due diligence and earnest monies in a timely manner. From the inspection costs to the appraisal fees, God gave us so much favor. The closing date was set for February 21st, 2020. The seller agreed to pay closing costs and we would have to pay $7800 in down payment fees. We were approved for $219,000 with a 3.5% down FHA Loan. I began praying immediately for a miracle because I had no family to get financial help from, and I was warned that it's against the law to take out a loan for down payment assistance, that only blood family members could help. God gave us a favor because, at a 613-credit score, we still qualified for the FHA loan. I was seeing

God moving on my behalf. I was praying so hard asking God to raise my score to 620 so that I would qualify for the down payment assistance the company offers. I asked the loan officer if we could use our tax return monies towards the down payment. She said yes. I continued to pray for a miracle because usually my return for the last seven years is always received that last week in February. I knew that our closing date was 2/21/2020. I had all of my children praying as well. I continued to pay my tithes and be faithful in my giving. We filed our taxes through H&R Block and for the first time in many years of filing, we decided to have our funds deposited directly into my bank account, instead of the usual HR Block emerald card. Usually, we would get a loan from our tax filing that same day onto their emerald card, and the rest would come at end of February on the 27th or 28th day. This year in 2020, we filed on January 31st a Friday. God answered our prayers, our tax return was direct deposited into my bank account on February 11th, 2020. I was at work and had to go into the bathroom as I worshipped and thanked God for intervening in the norm and sending that money early for us. I prayed for favor with the seller that she would be willing to sell some of the items that she owned that were very nice for a good price. My adult children that are working were willing to help us with their paychecks, to deposit into my account along with our refund to show proof of funds for closing. The process had to get final approval from the underwriter to close.

The realtor, Robert, called me and said that the seller wants to know if I am interested in her front load washer and dryer, her very nice silver colored barbeque propane grill, which sat outside under a huge metal awning that has plenty of storage space. Plus, her patio furniture, with coverings and cushions, and a fire pit, along with her other outdoor chairs and tables, along with other furniture that I admired during the tour. I told him absolutely.

The realtor called me again and asked me if we could close on Thursday 02/20/2020 instead of the 21st. My husband and I both agreed. The loan officer, Cassandra, said that this time was good for them as well. On Friday, Feb 14, 2020, I was able to print off my final requested bank statement and show proof of funds for closing. However, after that on the next day being Saturday, I paid my car note and the hotel fees for the upcoming week. I still needed a miracle. I no longer had $7800.00. Cassandra said that she gave our file over to the underwriter for its final approval. I checked my credit score again looking for a miracle. God spoke to me and told me to trust Him, that He has it under control. He said, "I am the God of all flesh, is there anything too hard for me?"

On Wednesday, I called Cassandra for the final number needed to close on the following morning. She told me initially that I would get the $500.00 appraisal fee back, and it would be deducted from my down payment cost. So, I was waiting for that final figure. I had $7,333.00 in my account. Cassandra called me and asked me if I had received the email with the final amount needed to close and to congratulate me because the underwriter had given the final approval to close in the morning.

When I opened up my email, I almost passed out, the exact amount in my account was the amount I read on the screen. $7,333.00. I felt like running all over that nurse's station. I HAD RECEIVED A MIRACLE. God had worked it all out.

Proudly and excitedly, on Thursday, 02/20/2020 we closed on our home. I was able to purchase the beautiful items from the seller at a very unbelievably reasonable price. My dream of owning a huge corner lot house with upstairs and downstairs and a pool had come true. This house is so huge and beautiful. It has a large pool with a deck, a gazebo, a she-shed, and a man cave. God is a miracle worker, a promise keeper, light in the darkness, our God that is who You are.

Never ever give up on your dreams. God is faithful to His word. He will make a way out of no way. Like Isaiah 43 says, he will make a way in the wilderness, and path rivers in the desert.

Be strong and know that God is always in control. The fact that we lived in the two hotel rooms for 83 days, paying $686.00 a week, caused me to use my credit cards a whole lot. By the time we closed, my credit score had really plummeted. I was in the low 600's. My fico score 8 was 650 plus, but the Mortgage score had dropped to the high 500's. I just ignored it and stopped checking my credit scores. I unsubscribed from myfico.com and Experian's daily update. My credit utilization went from 3% to 88%. I had been praying months prior, asking God for a total miracle in my scores, to remove those negative accounts. The letters I sent, requesting the accounts to be removed were in vain. They verified my accounts and the negatives were still on my report.

Well, in April of this year, I signed back into Experian and saw that my score had gone up six points. I was so happy and shocked. A week later I got a notification that my score went up again to 673. I looked more closely at my credit and saw that I had a message that those two negatives had been removed from my credit report. My credit utilization is lower now as well. My fico score 8 has gone up again this week. It is now 683. God is so good and faithful. He will fight for you and He will give you your heart's desires. Continue to pray and seek His face and always know that He is in control. God will cause men to give into your bosom.

Stay blessed in Jesus' name!

PASTOR GLENDA NEAL-LEGARDY: A LETTER OF ENCOURAGEMENT

Dear friend,

In the year 2016, September 16, I attended the women's conference at the church my husband and I attended. At one of the sessions, women were able to go and have prayer warriors pray with them and speak prophetically to them from God. I chose to go, and during my time with these women of God, a prophetic word was spoken to me about my life not being over. You see, prior to that conference (and I'll get back and share more what was said to me) I was questioning the Lord, "Have I gotten too old, am I doing my ministry correctly, am I missing something, what's happening?" Because I wasn't seeing the results of my labor like I thought I should. *Wow!*

I accepted the call of God to minister His word and to teach in 1998, before that, I was just happy to be saved. But, later as I continued growing in the Word and my ministerial training and using the spiritual gifts God gave me, the more confident I became. But, like many of us, we begin to wonder when we do not see progress, the fruits of our labor, and sometimes think the Lord is not with us. I must confess though, I did get in His way of what He was doing, impeding my progress. Then adding to that, I kept rehearsing in my mind, I'm getting older, here I was, now 66 years, and I felt I had not fulfilled my purpose yet.

Let me share the rest of God's word to me that evening. The Lord said He was pleased with me, and He will establish me in power and access for His Kingdom's purposes. That I was "to be encouraged," "the best is yet to come," and He said, He needs my time, my experiences, and my ministry. Another word of God came, and He said, "to rise up and breakout and I will be your rear guard, no longer feel as if your life is over, the best is yet to come." I was truly uplifted and blessed with God's word to me. The women that spoke the prophetic words to me did not know of my prayers and conversations that I had with the Father. He hears those that truly seek His will.

I wanted to share this life experience to encourage those who are in valleys of decisions or questioning what they should be doing with their lives, are they a failure, and like I did, think you are too old to accomplish goals, whatever they may be; first-time degree, job promotion, marriage, whatever it is. **We, of course, can do nothing independent of Jesus Christ (John 15:5 NIV).**

I am thriving in the ministry God has given me, as well as working alongside my husband.

As you seek the Lord, know that He is listening, knows your heart, and He is already working on your behalf. What He asks of us, as His children, and as we are called to serve, is faithfulness and obedience and trust in Him. **He will give us the desires of our hearts (Psalm37:4 NIV).**

For His Glory
Treasured Ministry
Life Koinonia Ministries

FIRST LADY MAVIS MCKNIGHT: THE GAG ORDER-THE VOICE THAT ALMOST WASN'T

I feel sad and shameful telling you this but here goes...When I was in my very early 20s, working one of my very first real jobs with the Los Angeles County Sherriff's Department, I found myself in a situation that changed my life forever. It felt like there was a gag over my mouth. Even now when I look back, I think about the agony of that ordeal. In a minute, I'll tell you how I got stuck in that situation, but first, let's go back in time.

I was raised by a very dominant Pastor's father. There were nine of us, four boys and five girls, and I was number six. My father was not far removed from slavery, but he didn't initially adopt the "do what I say and don't ask any questions, or you'll get beat" mentality. He was pretty lenient with the first third of us. My two older sisters and older brother were allowed to have an opinion, or "talk back." But once the last six landed on the airstrip, the "freedom of speech" era came to a screeching halt, and his reign of terror became our new norm. Instilling the fear of God in us with the use of a massive extension cord, became his customary practice.

That was the start of the "do what I say." "Don't talk back." "Get a beating or worse," mentality. Yep, those messages got deeply ingrained. We were always taught not to fight each other or anyone else or we would get a "beating" from our father. That impacted me heavily. My translation: Don't stand up for myself.

At ten years old, in 5th grade, this lesson materialized in living color. For no apparent reason that I could determine at the time, a young bully socked me dead in my stomach, hard. I let out a painful wail and cried, but never even told the teacher. I just stuffed down the pain, humiliation, and embarrassment; at ten years old! Still bothers me today.

When I went into 9th grade at 14 years old, I had found my best friend. She was outgoing and confident which was a contrast to my more subdued personality at the time. We both loved coffee cakes and loved to talk about boys. We also both had boyfriends that ran in the same circle. As the school year hit mid-semester, hormones were raging and most of the girls were giving up their panties to the boys. When my then-boyfriend approached me for sex, I was more afraid of my father than saying no to him. I said, "No." He said, "Okay, bet." He then asked my best girlfriend.

She said, "Yes," and she became his girlfriend without me ever knowing a thing about it! Although the agony of betrayal spread through me like wildfire, I never said a word to her or to him. I just stuffed down the pain, humiliation, and disappointment and thankfully found another friend.

By the time I was 18 years old, in a new meaningful relationship, I became acutely aware that the baggage of my past had shown up once again in my present
circumstance. I was caught in a family war zone, guns and fists ablaze, and became the target for their violence and anger. Although retaliating at that moment may have cost me my life, once it was all said and done and the apologies poured in, I eagerly accepted them, and just stuffed down pain, humiliation, and disrespect.
But I wasn't done yet.

I was now 20 years old, and life had gotten a lot better. I felt good and ready for my next chapter. I was just getting started in the workforce and loved my job with the L.A. County Sherriff's Department. After a few months, a co-worker asked me out, I accepted, and we soon started dating.

About a month later he invited me on a weekend getaway, all expenses paid. I jumped at the chance. We hopped in his car, headed down the highway, and landed in Tijuana, Mexico; Checked into the hotel, hit the hottest club spots; Partied hard, drank much, and enjoyed the nightlife to the fullest.

Once back at the hotel he expected sex. The kissing starts, then intensifies, then he grabs and squeezes my breasts with way too much aggression. This is his idea of "foreplay" which takes a whopping three minutes!

Without delay or concern for me, he commences shoving his finger into my Lady Bits, ramming it in and out like a pile-driver trying to break up concrete! This wasn't like the movies. This didn't feel good. This felt horrible! Over and over, he rammed his fist into my sacred space, and with every slam, I flinched. The worst part was he never even noticed. He soon plunged into the sex act, and it was the same throughout the entire ordeal.

I wasn't that experienced, but I knew it wasn't supposed to feel like this. While the words, "PLEASE STOP!" screamed inside my head, not a peep escaped from my lips. I just laid there, suffered in silence, and endured the excruciating pain. The negative messages I heard growing up were not promising It started with: You should be seen and not heard. Your voice doesn't matter. Your needs don't matter. You have no power.

When I hear these messages inside my head, I can feel the weight on my heart. I surely wasn't doing myself any favors by holding onto these beliefs. But my past didn't determine my future. This was evident in what happened next. The following morning, he wanted more, and before I could stop myself, the word "NO!" flew out of my mouth! I was in so much pain I could hardly walk that day. At that very moment, I decided I would never, ever, let anyone dishonor, devalue, or disrespect my sacred Queen again. My motto became, "I don't do, plain!" I was ready for something new and lasting.

Although that experience taught me to speak up for what I wanted and didn't want, my transformation didn't happen right away. However, I certainly didn't wait for my vulva to be bushwhacked again before I made a move. You see, part of a fear of speaking up is you have no knowledge of what you're speaking up about. So, I first had to ask myself *was it my dignity? Was it my own personal worth? Was it learning what sex was all about? Was it learning to believe sex was truly better than what I had experienced? Was I embarrassed to learn what turned me on? Was I ashamed of learning my own body's capacity for pleasure?* These questions pushed me toward my quest to discover my voice and to also learn about the joys and pleasures of sex. My journey has had its challenges. In the beginning, it wasn't all peaches, cream, and roses. I struggled. It took some time for me to build up the courage to speak up for myself. I learned about affirmations. Positive thinking.

HOW TO BE MORE ASSERTIVE

No matter how many times I had to repeat, recite, or reaffirm to strengthen my backbone, I did it because I was determined to step into a new way of thinking, feeling, and being. The coolest thing about this journey was finding my voice outside of the bedroom, as well as finding my voice inside of the bedroom. Today, I can speak candidly and effortlessly about my bedroom needs and desires, likes, and dislikes. I even look forward to being satiated and satisfied in my sexual experiences and I couldn't be more thrilled! Even though my journey has been filled with hills, valleys, ups, downs, joys, failures, and triumphs, I stuck with it and didn't give up. I am now unshackled and wrapped in a blanket of excitement and will always cherish my newfound discovery: Turning "the voice that almost wasn't" into "the voice that forever will be!"

THE BEAUTY OF THE GAG ORDER

Your first thought may be, *how is a gag order a beautiful thing?* Simply this. It was not your doing, so you have the permission and power to remove it! Once removed, you can say with courage and confidence, that "I am in charge of my voice, and I am forever empowered to use it to speak up for me, my needs and desires, and my future!"

Mavis McKnight, MS is a Certified Sex Coach, Marriage Advocate, and a Pastor's wife, who is passionate about teaching women to add flavor and spice to their sex life, blend sex positive messages with actions, and create tantalizing sexual experiences that burst with sweetness. You can connect with her at askmavis@mavismcknight.com. You can also visit her website at www.mavismcknight.com to learn more about who she is, what she does, and who she serves.

LIFE STORY OF EVANGELIST SYLVIA R. WILKERSON

My name is Evangelist Sylvia R. Wilkerson, I was born in Los Angeles, California on February 13, 1963. At the age of 27, I had a life-changing experience with rheumatoid arthritis from February 12, 1991, until 2008. My sons were nine years old, 20 months old, and my only baby girl was six months old. I would like to share how God gave me the strength and determination to overcome this attack of rheumatoid arthritis on my body physically and mentally.

My symptoms started with a fever that would only occur at night when I would go to bed. I prayed over myself and believed God would heal me. I thought it was just a little virus trying to attack me. I took over-the-counter medicine for the fever and continued to stay hydrated. I thought it would pass in a few days. After a week or two of experiencing the fever episodes every night, my feet and knee joints started feeling like they were on fire, and red burning itching whelps began to appear all over my body.

I couldn't wear shoes because my feet became swollen with fluid. It became difficult to use my hands to do easy tasks around the house. The spirits of depression, oppression, hopelessness, anger, and complaining took a grip on me. My children were babies, two were in diapers and on bottles. I thank God my husband was there to help me, but emotionally it was a challenge because I was the wife and mother of my household and I felt defeated in my body.

I went to urgent care, and the doctors could not find out or determine what it was. This attack mimicked many different immune diseases.

I am a very strong-willed woman and being a child of God I refused to accept defeat. This was an attack that required all my faith, strength, and total trust in God to overcome this physical battle. I was referred to a rheumatologist. I went through numerous blood tests, x-rays, and then there were different kinds of medications I was prescribed. I was taking the medications, following the doctor's orders and recommendations, but my condition was getting worse.

This attack went on for years. The doctor's appointments were just a waste of time. I kept confessing and believing in God for my complete healing. I never had a pity party. I kept a smile on my face in front of my kids. I wanted to be an example of being strong in my faith for my children while fighting the excruciating pain attacking the joints in my body.

I became angry with the doctors because they started giving me pain medications which became a band-aid and not a solution to the problem. I did not feel comfortable lying in bed, while my children were up and active. I enjoyed interacting with them. I pushed myself to do simple things; combing my daughter's hair, stand up and cook dinner, and walk around outside for a few hours with my kids.

The depression was setting in and I could not let it control me. I was quoting and reading every scripture I could find on healing, depression, loneliness, you name it, I read it and quoted it. Then I began to think, with the help of Satan, "Maybe God is punishing me for not being where I should be spiritually in my ministry and that could be the reason, I was suffering from this condition for so many years." The devil was having a field day with my mind, but the small still voice of Jesus would remind me what the word of God says about the thief.

God blessed me to move my children from Los Angeles to North Hollywood. My children were ages 13, five, and four years old. I was determined not to let this attack on my body stop me. I would get up, feet swollen most mornings, holding on to the walls to hold my balance and walk. It was difficult to use a cane, my hands and wrists were swollen and inflamed most of the time. I helped my husband prepare breakfast and assisted with getting my children to get ready for school. This normal activity would leave me drained physically and emotionally and I weighed only 105 pounds.

Some days I would wake up and be in so much pain. I would wake up angry, fighting depression, thoughts of suicide, and mad that Satan was attacking me. I knew this was an attack from Satan. Just to give him a black eye, I would leave the house early, drive my children to school, and walked them onto the schoolyard, limping in pain.

I had a husband and three children to take care of. My children were school age and I refused to allow the physical attack on my body to stop me from participating in my children's educational growth as a normal active mom. I began to get up with the kids, get dressed, and take them to school. It was very painful at first, but I kept telling myself, "I can do all things through Christ, who strengthens me."

After a week or two, I began to volunteer at my children's elementary school. I felt being productive to help the innocent kids at school would take my mind off from how I was feeling. And it did! It was a blessing being around those little innocent faces. I began to learn that ministry was not just standing over the pulpit ministering to adults, there were also little children who needed ministering to as well.

The children were hungry for someone to show them patience, compassion, and encouragement. Most of their parents were single moms, and the school was a daycare for them. God allowed me to volunteer in various classrooms. I went to a parent meeting, and I noticed there was no parent participation. I had compassion for the Bolivian lady who was trying to conduct the meeting with no cooperation from the parents at all. She was shy, soft-spoken, and unable to effectively provide the parents with the information they were requesting. I took notes during the meeting that I thought would be helpful for her at the next meeting.

After the meeting, I introduced myself to her and a new friendship began. She had a nonprofit organization which was functioning illegally on the school campus. God gave us favor with an attorney, who assisted us with information on how to file for a 501.c3 for a nonprofit organization.

We successfully filed for our 501.c3, received our Employee Identification Number, and began to have our fundraisers on the school campus. God blessed us to have successful fundraisers. We raised funds to provide the teachers and students with materials, sponsored field trips and other needs in areas the school district did not provide funding.

I found my purpose during that time! I was so thankful to God leading me to the right place at the right time. God showed me how to get the parents involved by showing them the love and compassion of Christ in me. It was a blessing to meet so many women of all races and nationalities with the same concerns and need. Which was Christ in their lives. I was able to share my testimony about the attack I was experiencing with the Rheumatoid Arthritis. The parents were amazed and knew it was God because they would see me at the school every day with my cane, volunteering my time.

God blessed me to have favor with the principal of the school, the teachers, students, and all the parents. I became well known and respected at my children's school. I was offered a job at the school, and I had to respectfully decline due to the demands of the position and my physical limitations at the time.

It was a blessing to be helpful to so many of God's people. It was a blessing to see that I still had a purpose despite my physical limitations. God saw me through a successful surgery on my right wrist due to the Arthritis, but I immediately returned to the school, in bandages ready to volunteer. Volunteering became my therapy, purpose, and ministry at that time in my life. The word of God says that "His ways are not our ways, neither are His thoughts our thoughts." I learned that to be true. The way I thought God was going to deliver me did not happen at all.

The Word of God says, "Suffer the little children to come unto me for such is the Kingdom of Heaven." God allowed hundreds of little children at a school to help me overcome oppression, depression, suicidal thoughts, and the physical attack I was experiencing. I became so involved in helping the children and their parents that I would forget to take my medicine for the arthritis because I was not focusing on the pain.

After months of forgetting to take the medication, I stopped taking it. I noticed the pain was not as severe, and I could manage it. I weaned myself totally off my addiction to pain medication with the help of the Holy Spirit guiding me. I cried out to God many nights asking, "Why me?" and I learned, why not me? God blessed me to plant seeds in many children and their parents. I give all glory, honor, and praise to God for totally healing my body. I have not taken any kind of medication for Rheumatoid Arthritis in 20 years or so.

The power of God is amazing and never ceases to amaze me. God blessed our organization to help families of children who attended school every year for five years. Since then, God has blessed me to go to college and get my AA in Business and a bachelor's degree in human services management. I am a Licensed Evangelist, a notary for the state of Nevada, and working towards my notary signing agent certification. With God all things are possible, we just must believe. God has no respect of person.

GEORGETTE LAWRENCE:
ADOPTION...IT'S A GOOD THING

I was adopted in July of '64. I had wonderful parents and their version of love made me want the same. Because I was adopted, though I was well-loved, I still wanted my own family, one that had same bloodline with me. Both of my parents died while I was young, that made the longing for a family and child more extreme. I wanted a family, one from my own womb. It never dawned on me that I would have to struggle and ultimately give up my dream.

I married a handsome young man in the summer of 1990. Hoping, praying, and wishing for the love and security that I found in my parents' home. It did not quite work out that way. Barely six months before we got married, a woman said she was pregnant with my husband's baby. I learned that the enemy will use what you desire the most to attack and kill your dream if he can. I remember being devastated. This was nowhere close to what I desired in my marriage. About a year into the marriage, I took a pregnancy test one day and the line was pink. *I was pregnant.* Finally, I was ecstatic and went about the next month and a half in bliss. After I came home from work one day, I started to bleed. I prayed as hard and long as I could, *please don't let me lose this baby.*

My ex-husband and I went to the hospital, the doctor said I had a spontaneous abortion. My heart was hurt, but my ex-husband assured me that I would get pregnant again, and I believed him. A few months later, I was pregnant again. I was excited but nervous. I did not want to tell anyone because I did not want something to happen. Once again, I started to bleed except this time, my ex-husband would not take me to the hospital. He chose to hang with his friends. I had to call my aunt for her to drive me to the hospital. She was not pleased, and I could not blame her. Unfortunately, it colored her perception of him, and I did not have the energy to change it. I was mad and hurt because I couldn't imagine I would let someone treat me like that. Our marriage had serious problems.

A couple of years passed, and I still was not pregnant. I could not understand what was going on, I should have been pregnant by now. I became depressed. I hated making love and even taking the steps that the doctor advised I would need to take afterwards. Even though we had moved from where we lived, I was again facing my husband telling me another woman was pregnant by him. I thought, *Lord how can this be*, still, I was not ready to give up on my marriage. I was holding on to it like it was a life raft on a sinking ship. Eventually, the ship sailed without me on it, and yes, when it sailed, the new girlfriend was pregnant.

I was single, no dating prospects, and no child. Year after year passed, yet there was no change. I had a short-term relationship with a man that I met and could not believe that I was pregnant from our first encounter. In my mind, this was it. This was not the way God handles things, but it was what I wanted. God finally had given me my heart's desire. I was pregnant. I was so excited that I decided to go out with some friends to Louisiana to the Essence Festival. I was having an awesome time when suddenly I started bleeding. I went to the hospital and the doctor says, "I can't tell if you are miscarrying because your HCG (Human chorionic gonadotropin) levels are not high enough, go back home and see your regular doctor." I did as he told me. The doctor then said he wanted to watch me for a few days and if my levels continue to go up, we were good. I kept getting blood work done and miraculously, my levels kept going up. *Everything was going fine*. One day I went to work, the bleeding started again, and my secretary drove me to the hospital. Initially, the doctor said that he heard the heartbeat. I was so excited. "You do?" I asked. Surprisingly, he went silent and the next thing he said was "I don't see a baby, just the sack. You can expect for it to pass within the next few days and if it does not, we will have to give you a D&C." *How can that be?* How can you hear a heartbeat one minute and see nothing the next? Once more, I was devastated and crying so hard that one of the nurses opened a private room so that I would not disturb the other patients. As I cried, my secretary tried to comfort me, but I was inconsolable. I remembered something I saw on TV once, where a lady told her teenage daughters that fairy tales did not happen for black women, that it simply wasn't our reality. At that moment, that thought was solidified in my heart. I took that as my mantra.

Life went on, and after some female problems, my OB/GYN said I needed a hysterectomy. That was when I knew my dream of having a family was dead. Not only did I not have a husband, but I also had no prospects of one, and now, I had no womb. I went into a deep depression.

My cousin said to me, "Why don't you adopt?"

"No, I do not want to adopt." I was adamant about having my own child from my own womb and that was no longer an option. So, I would live my life, childless. I said it with such force that she said was "okay," and never mentioned it again. In 2006, I had the hysterectomy and I moved on with my life. I was tired of crying over it. I was done. This is my reality.

Fast Forward Three Years Later

I normally spent Thanksgiving with my friend and her family. This year, I just didn't want to do it. I was going to stay home by myself the whole Thanksgiving weekend. I wasn't sad, I just wanted to be alone *even though I was already alone*. Faith Hill and her husband were having a special show on adoption. For some reason, I was drawn to that show. I don't remember setting out to watch it so, I must have just stumbled across it. I watched so many children ask for someone to love them and take care of them, and so many childless couples and singles offer that love and support. It made me think, *I have love to give why not give it to someone who needs it*. It may not look like I wanted it to look but it was still love. Everyone wants love. By the end of the show, my heart was changed. I called child services that night. *Thanksgiving night*. I left a voicemail that I was interested in becoming a foster parent. That Monday, I received a call back that the foster care program for new parents would not begin until January of 2010.

As an act of faith, in December, I bought two beautiful Christmas ornaments, one for both children I would receive. See, I had decided that I was going to ask for sibling girls, and I was hoping they would be around the ages of two or three. Siblings, because I didn't want anyone else to experience what I did as an only child with no immediate family close or really engaged, with me. Mind you, I have always wanted boys and when anyone would ask me about having children, I would say I wanted boys. In this case, in my wisdom, I decided I'd better get girls because at least, I can relate to them about growing up. Boys need a man around, and I don't have that to give them. Girls do too, but I thought I could work with that. Also, back during the time of my separation from my ex-husband, the Lord spoke to my spirit that I would have sons. I kept that in my heart, but I must be honest, I released it when I had the hysterectomy. *I released it but God honors his word*.

During the time that I took the training to become a foster parent, the company I worked for was in contract negotiations. One of the requirements for the foster care system is a home inspection. So, even though I had completed the course, I did not immediately sign up for the home inspection. I did not want to share my time with the company if I received a child. Months went by and the contract negotiations kept stalling. In June, I decided that if I kept putting this off, the year will come to an end, and I won't have what I wanted because of the company.

On July 8th, I called to schedule my home inspection. Because of the recession at the time, the inspector told me that he could not come in the month of July, that I would have to schedule for August. I was fine with that. I took my two weeks of vacation and came back to work. On August 6th, the inspector came to my house and gave me the *home approval*. I could officially accept foster children. On August 12th, I received a call from my social worker, she had a child that she wanted to place with me. It was an infant. I said no, I don't want an infant, I want a two-year-old.

I asked the social worker if I could think about it and she said, "Yes, but not long because we want to get him bonded, he is only three days old." I tried calling everyone that was close to me, that knew my situation, so that, I could get some advice. No one answered their phone. *I mean NO ONE!* One of my coworkers came to my office and I asked for a walk as I explained the situation to her.

"You should not take him, he needs a dad," she said, and the more reasons she gave me not to take him, the more peace settled in my heart that I should take him.

I told the social worker I would call her back by 1:00. I called her back only one hour later to say, "Yes, I will take him." She then told me the baby has been safely surrendered, he had no drugs in his system. He was healthy and would be eligible for me to adopt him after six months.

I asked her what his name is, and she said, "He doesn't have one, you will be able to name him." God gave me the desire of my heart. I had a brand-new healthy baby that I did not have to birth. *That was rare for everyone involved.* He is my blessing from the Lord, that maketh rich and addeth no sorrow. When I look at him, I know God can and will do what he said. It's not always in our timing and it's not always the way we want it, but he orders my steps. Everything about the circumstances of my little boy was perfect down to the daycare being right across the street from me. *That's another story.* It's ironic I am completing this on Mother's Day. For the naysayers, God gave me a second son as well, *just as much a miracle as the first one.* I'm blessed and living a life I never thought I would. God is good, all the time.

APOSTLE ALICIA GEORGE:
GETTING OFF ON THE WRONG FLOOR

O nce a queen, always a queen. I was crowned school queen of my high school in 1973. I was asked to represent my class and run for the coveted title of Miss C.A.H.S. queen, in St. Thomas, Virgin Islands, where I was born. It was right after that, I realized that one of my best friends decided to run because I was running. I realized then, that there was always someone around, trying to make me feel second best. I remembered always being called Irma's sister, *never my name*. It was at that time of my high school years I seemed to start searching for something of my own identity.

I have experienced hurt, betrayal, and love on many level – in and out of the church, in and out of marriage. This led me to a private, promiscuous life that led me to years of secret drug abuse and thoughts of suicide and murder. I became very good at hiding stuff from the world and from myself.

It was important to be able to recover. I moved to New York from St. Thomas, Virgin Islands, right out of high school. New York had never been anywhere out of reckoning when I was looking for adventure and education. Reality set in when it did not go that way and I had to get a real job. I experienced getting fired because I did not type fast enough to keep up with the demands of the job. That became my second bout with low self-esteem. Thinking back over those days, steered me to writing my third book *Self Esteem* available on Amazon.

Ladies With Purpose

I remember being chased by a young man in high school, and in my New York days, being told, "you are going to be my girlfriend, and have my baby." I did not like him. He was too militant.

I was going to become a court reporter. However, when that did not happen, I looked at it as another way life had failed my dreams. I remember being so upset about not making that dream come to pass that I just decided dreams don't really apply to me.

I began sleeping around, something I said I would never do. *Never say never*. It was one of those night parties, listening to the good old music of the 70's that introduced me to cocaine. You see, up until then, it was just smoking weed every day, and getting on the E-train to work. By this time, I had an excellent job making good money, a nice apartment living a double life.

The journey took me back to the Virgin Islands after I realized I was not a snow baby. Beaches, sun, and fun were more of who I was. Well, that militant young man kept his promise to himself. He found me there, and sure enough, I had his baby. I took work because of my past. It seemed that I would never be able to have a child, but the militant prophet spoke it and had a plan.

I laid on my back with my feet tied with a belt to the doorknob for hours, after one of our passionate nights, and boom, the next month I was pregnant with my only living child. You see, there were miscarriages, abortions, and God knew I could not handle more than one. The tremor teenage abuse still lingered in at the back of my mind, hidden from the world and those that knew me.

That cocaine habit was later upgraded to a crack habit, *initiated by another sleeping partner*. I thought it was a secret until it became a daily part of my life that led to more men. One of the men became my supplier. I did not have to pay for my own load because I could sell it for him too. This was a man even in a million years, I would never give a second look because he was not my type or what I considered *on my level*. Pride was always lurking in the background and waiting until the right time to show up.

Ladies With Purpose

Then he came into my life on a pair of skates. He had the nerve to skate right into my job with green shorts and thunder thighs with a smile that reminded me the sun will shine again. We did not waste time we engaged in a hot and fiery romance, then came the separation. Once all of his baggage was exposed, he disappeared and twelve years later, he would re-enter my life to become my husband. I said hot and fiery romance, also a hot and fiery marriage. It was a storm brewing, waiting to become a category five hurricane.

His past collided with my past and we both became oil and water. We were both serving God but, with very different relationships with our Father. I knew on the day of my wedding there was still time to say no. *It was all planned, how do I get out of this.* Confirmation came the night prior to our wedding when two of my girlfriends that flew in for my wedding shared what I did not want to see or hear. Drugs were all over him, but I chose to close my eyes to that and got married with my eyes wide open. Yep, I remembered how great the fire used to be and I wanted to feel the burn again. It had been so many years of not being intimate with a man. You see, I was saved for real and loved God with all my heart.

The storm started almost on the wedding night. He was happy but acted kind of strange. I came to the reality after that was because he was high. I braced myself up for more because in the back of my mind I could make him change. After all, the fire was still in the bed. He was always a very corporate and IBM kind of man. I never saw one paycheck and did not know how much he made in our nine years of marriage. *Warning signs you shouldn't ignore from the start.* I learned at an early age to be independent. You see, I knew about my dad going to work at sea for months which meant to me, my mom independent.

There were the fights that became battles. We would verbally tear each other apart for the first two years like a slowly moving storm and then, we moved into category three, hurricanes. It was always drugs, jail, and then recovery for him.

Ladies With Purpose

When category five came, it was pushing, screaming, and then hitting. Well, I did not forget that the first three letters in my name were A-L-I, so, I learned how to punch right back. We were still working high profile jobs, and by then, he was a pastor and building a church, yet trading in drugs, but not dealing with the true hurt of rejection – that rejection that lurked within him.

The nights were long, and the days were short, pretending to be happy was taking its toll on me, so, I started taking longer trips for my work and booking trips that were not necessary so that I did not have to be around him. I loved the church and the people of God, but the pressure of home was always a secret storm. You see, we looked great together. He was charismatic and charming, but he was a character and I kept trying to fix him. But how can you fix someone when you needed to be fixed yourself?

Well, there was about to be a perfect storm. I started doing what I heard God say I should do. I started doing women's conferences, Covenant Whole Women. The first year, I was speaking on the stage, and I heard myself telling everything that was so secret about my past, the drugs, the sexual promiscuity, the abuse, the money, I told it all then. In the end, women who had the same secrets came to the altar because they had secrets also. It was like, let the healing begin! Whoops, there it was, like Aretha Franklin said R-E-S-P-E-C-T. Up until then, I was searching for it.

By now, my skills of defense as ALI had been perfected. There was evidence of rough and abusive nights, but morning always came, and I can pretend again that all was well. I decided I did not want to pretend any longer and I was tired of being in this hurricane. So, now was the time for an earthquake; there had to be a shaking. I planned what I would do because I remembered a story the "militant" once told me, so I decided to put it to a test. I would let the pastor go to sleep. I would heat cooking oil until I knew it was at the temperature of a volcano. I would plan to pour it in his ear and fry his brain.

I started up the stairs with the oil and on about the third or fourth step I heard, *"So, to be clear, when he is dead and you're spending your life in prison, how does God get the glory?"*

I backed down the stairs, mourning. I knew that the hurricane, earthquake, and volcano had created the perfect storm and it was over. I wanted out, and he knew it was time he filed for the divorce. The only thing left was our last name being the same, and he decided he wanted that back. The name means COVENANT. *By the way, I still use it when needed, after all I earned it.*

God took me to a place of remembrance of years that I had chosen not to confront the pains and hurts of the past that I kept suppressed and not dealt with. It was not all him, I had lots of demons that I must confront. I sat in a church for over a year and allowed God to heal the tornado of things that had been going round and round in my mind, destroying everything that got in the way without identifying the real source. He allowed me to give birth to all those dead babies and He Renewed my Life. I pastored Renewed Life Worship Center for twelve years in California, and now, I know it is time to return to the beaches, sun and fun to be crowned as a queen on the island and renew the quiet storm that has been brewing for years. To dream big and know that dreams do come to pass, but then, you get to choose which one.

It was all preparing me for what I was going to walk into. It was all necessary to get me to where I am today. When the past and future collide, it produces jewels. It brought me to wearing my crown straight and not leaning on the side with a sapphire that signifies my birth.

LAWANDA FORD:
STRIVE TO PERSEVERE

I was born and raised in South Central Los Angeles, California in 1965, to the proud parents of Jeanette Parnell and Leon Turner. I was born the fifth child of six. I have four sisters and one brother. My parents were not married at the time of my birth. Before the age of three, my parents terminated their relationship and before the age of four, my mother, being a single mom of six, had a nervous breakdown. My siblings and I were placed in foster care. We were placed in separate foster homes for a short time. Meanwhile, my grandparents, Jean and John Edwards, had petitioned the courts for legal guardianship of me and my siblings. Thereafter, we lived and was raised by our grandparents.

I attended Normandie Avenue Elementary School. I was always a bright student and the teacher's pet. One of the fondest memories in elementary school was being a member of the Normandie Avenue stepperette drill team. We were an award-winning, prominent drill team in Los Angeles and a force to be reckoned with. My close friends were in the magnet class. I was tested but did not pass. My best friend was Carolyn Bell.

My grandmother passed away when I was in the 5th grade. I was too young to really grasp the seriousness and gravity of her passing, and the grief my grandfather certainly was experiencing.

I attended Horseman Jr. High School. I was enrolled in mostly magnet classes. I was a good and studious student. I was a cheerleader, played softball, and volleyball. I was also in a dance group with my friends known as *The Parliament Supremes*. We danced within the 7th, 8th, and 9th grade talent shows, placing each year. I was elected "best dancer" by my classmates.

Ladies With Purpose

I became a Crenshaw High School Cougar in 1979. I was very studious. I was a straight A student. I didn't participate in any extracurricular activities. My grandfather passed away when I was in the 10th grade. My siblings and I raised ourselves from that point. Thank God for the foundation that our grandparents instilled in us. I was elected "most likely to succeed" by my peers for the senior most. I graduated in 1983, fourteenth in my class, an honor student with a 4.0 GPA.

As far as college is concerned, I believe that I did not receive the proper guidance, counsel, education nor preparation for college. I was accepted to UC Berkeley and Occidental College without even applying. I knew nothing about the value of college, so I applied and elected to attend college at California State University, Dominguez Hills because that's where some of my friends were going. I enjoyed the college experience. I was affiliated with the Phi Beta Sigmas. I was a Sigma Dove. Unfortunately, I only attended college for one year. I decided to, *in my infinite wisdom*, drop out of college and get a job.

My first job was as a Data Entry Operator, at Northrop Gruman in 1984. I worked in aerospace for six years. Thereafter, I started a twenty-five-year career in the apparel manufacturing industry. I held the following positions: receptionist, administrative assistant, executive assistant, sales assistant, production manager assistant, and production manager. During these twenty-five-years, I acquired a very specific and professional skill set. There are not too many African Americans in the apparel manufacturing industry, so I felt that I had to represent and dispel all stereotypes about African Americans' existence in each of the companies where I worked. I worked hard, excelled, and was promoted. I owe to my former employers a great deal of gratitude for the professional skill sets that I acquired in their employment. I would say that my greatest skills are communication, written, verbal, organization, detail, follow up, and follow-through skills. However, at some point, I felt as though my career was not fulfilling. As I grew older and matured, I came to believe that there were more pressing matters in the world that I would rather invest my time, passion, and professionalism in, rather than that which I was investing in the production of a blouse, a pair of pants, a handbag, etc.

In 2008, our country experienced a financial crisis which destroyed many businesses and brought grave losses to millions of Americans. The apparel industry was hit hard. I was finally laid off in 2013 when the company closed. In watching my favorite news program, CNN, many of the guest speakers would share stories of how many Americans were also laid off and losing their livelihoods and jobs and were forced to reinvent themselves in order to survive. I thought to myself, *what could I do to reinvent myself? How could I best use my professional skill sets (communication, written, verbal, organization, detail, and follow up, and follow-through skills) to become a self-employed entrepreneur? Legal services*, I thought. I thought that starting a company in legal services would be fulfilling to me, as I would be helping people resolve some very important, very personal, very sensitive, and life-altering and disputed matters in their lives at a reasonable fee. I began to research the industry and certification requirements.

In January 2014, I started my own business, *Merit Legal Services*. Starting my own business was exciting. I knew that there was a need for my service at a reasonable fee to people who could not afford to retain an attorney. I was convinced that my business would take off immediately. I was wrong. I had to return to the apparel industry twice to have an income while I established my business. Hence, I worked a full-time job, then came home and worked my business nights and weekends. It was tiring and exhausting but totally worth it. I was determined and driven to have my business succeed. Finally, in 2018, my business and clientele were soundly established and self-sustaining. The year, 2019, was the best fiscal year for my business to date.

I have secured a devoted client base, using my professional skillset, personable attention, and excellent customer service provided in each case and to every client. I work hard and long, days, nights, and weekends. I am determined and motivated to succeed. I will retire as a self-employed professional.

To date, I have not married, and I have no children, however, I am complete in Christ who has blessed me with a number of siblings; ten nephews, one niece, 15 great-nephews, 17 great-nieces, and a host of friends. I have acquired life-long friends from Elementary School, Jr. High School, High School, and College, of which I still have a relationship with. Those that I have lost contact with causes me to be sad because I have come to learn that *the most important things in life are family and friends*.

The message I leave to you is: We have no control over the circumstances we are born into, but we must strive to persevere and overcome those hindering things from our past, through faith, knowledge, family and friends. We must heal from our past lest we allow our past to cripple our future. Focus on your strengths, dream big, plan, and execute.

God Bless You

MINISTER BJ BIKER CHIC:
EARLY SUNDAY MORNING

Early Sunday morning, I slowly crawled out of bed, hoping he wouldn't hear me and wake up. My body was pumping so much adrenaline that my heart rate sped up to 110.1 beats per minute (average heart rate when scared). All night, I heard voices telling me to *come home, you're better than this, I created you for so much more.* I had no idea why these vocal utterances were in my head, but all I knew was that I had to leave this volatile lifestyle before I go insane and become mentally deranged.

FRATERNITY RUSH WEEK

I met Frankie during fraternity rush week, where he was pledging, and where I signed up to be an Alpha Angel. As quiet and shy as I was, I had no idea what compelled me to become an Alpha Angel. Alpha Angels were considered the pledges little sisters, and it was our responsibility to assist them during their six weeks of pledging. Our duties consisted of washing their clothes, cooking for them, hiding them out so they could rest from their brutal and nonsensical pledging activities. Frankie and I became very close during the pledging period, so we started going out after he "crossed the line." Life was good, and dating was fun! Since we both lived in the dorms, we spent a lot of time in each other's room studying, and on the weekends, I usually cooked a seven-bone roast, which was his favorite.

Frankie and I were the perfect couple! He was a short glass of "cold ice-tea" on a hot summer day, and I was a cute "vanilla wafer." We were the perfect match. His build was similar to an incredible miniature hulk, and I was stacked like a "Brick House" (36/24/36). I wore miniskirts to class, and he wore bow ties. It was as if he stepped out of a GQ magazine, and I stepped out of Vogue. In the early '80s, this is how we dressed. Nowadays, college students wear jeans, t-shirts, and tank tops.

Since Frankie and I were both from southern California, we spent a lot of time together over our school breaks. While we were living on campus in the dorms, we were limited to what we could do because we had roommates. When we went home during school breaks, we had more private time together, and this is where he began to show me his other side and our relationship took an odd turn.

GOING DOWN HILL

In 1983, during my 3rd year in college, I decided to move into an apartment. Frankie and I's relationship began to get a little rocky. One night while still living in the dorms, we got into a big argument, which resulted in a break-up. I was so furious. I started yelling, which made things a lot worse. While we were standing in the hall in front of his dorm room, he slapped me so hard, I heard a ringing in my ear, and my head started spinning. Hitting a black woman in the face is the worst thing he could have done. Once I came to my senses, realizing what happened, I pounced onto him like a hungry tiger going after her prey for the kill. I could feel my claws tearing into his skin as I emphatically screamed, "what the hell is your problem, I will kill you." I swung and yelled, swung, and yelled until I was tired, then left the room. That night, I tried to commit suicide because the person that I thought was the love of my life broke my heart by breaking up with me.

After spending the night in the ER and having my stomach pumped due to the suicide attempt, I woke the next day as if nothing ever happened. I bounced back so quickly that I completely forgot what happened the night before. I erased Frankie from my memory bank and moved on with my studies. Rather than focus on what I lost, I started focusing more on me and my education. Our separation didn't last too long. Since our break-up, Frankie's grades began to tank since he was heartbroken, so we reconciled, and nine months later, I found myself lying on a hospital bed with my legs in stirrups having an abortion.

NOT GOOD ENOUGH

After having an abortion, my life emotionally took a turn for the worst. I started feeling guilty, ashamed, and depressed over what I did. I murdered an innocent baby without giving him or her the chance to defend herself. Since Frankie and I were the only people that knew, I suppressed my feelings and acted like nothing ever happened. After moving into my apartment, I found myself falling deeper into a state of mental anguish. Having an abortion was one thing but having sex with Frankie was degrading. He enjoyed taking me to porno films and performing as if we were in the movie when we got home. I felt so awful and dirty that I resorted to smoking weed to hide the pain. I felt like I was losing my mind, especially since he started talking about a threesome. Having sex with Frankie was one thing, but the thought of including a third person was horrific. It would appear I was not good enough since he needed more stimulation.

THE PAINFUL REALITY

The summer of '83 I needed to escape before losing my mind. Even though I was not a born-again believer, I knew my life was not going in the right direction. I needed to act quickly otherwise, I was headed for the streets as a prostitute, since I felt my saneness slowly slipping away. My university had a summer ROTC program that I quickly signed up for, and for six long rugged weeks of climbing walls, rappelling down buildings, shooting M16s, push-ups, and cadence marches, I was back to my old self again: confident, fortified, and fierce!

BACK TO SCHOOL

Summer was just about over, and I was ready to begin a new school semester. Heading to the bookstore to purchase new textbooks, I bumped into a friend that could not wait to fill me in on all the juicy gossip about Frankie while I was away at ROTC boot camp. Frankie was driving my convertible with a girl in the passenger seat. She was seen leaving his apartment early in the morning, and they were spotted snuggling close on campus. Since school was about to start, I was too busy to address Frankie's extracurricular activities, so I shrugged it off.

On the first day of the fall semester, I was excited. I had an apartment, a new bike, and a new roommate, life couldn't be any better. I planned to see Frankie after class to catch up and see how his summer went. I figured we'd grab a bite to eat, have sex, and talk about the fun things we did over the summer, but all that came to a screeching halt when I saw them. I couldn't believe my eyes. My friend was right! I saw Frankie walking with a girl, holding her textbooks in one hand while his other hand-held hers. I was horrified! A sharp pain shot through my body while my heart dropped to my feet. My throat felt like the Mojave Desert, and as quickly as I could, I made a U-turn. I couldn't believe it! He was seeing someone else and didn't have the nerve to tell me it was over.

Heart-broken for the first time, and not knowing what to do, I called my mom. I was crushed with sorrow and wanted to kill myself since my life was over, *so I thought*. I cried so hard that my mom couldn't understand what I was saying over the phone. By the time I finished crying, killing myself was out of the question. She convinced me that I had a beautiful life ahead of me and not to let one man ruin it.

The next morning, I went to his apartment, he opened the door, but wouldn't let me in. Looking over his shoulder, I saw the hat his new girlfriend wore when I spotted them walking together on campus-she was in his apartment. I tried to force my way into his apartment, but he kept pushing me back. I pleaded with Frankie not to break off our relationship, but he pushed me out of his doorway into the hallway and slammed the door in my face. The pain I felt was excruciating. I have never been so humiliated in my life. I felt used, taken for granted, filthy, abandoned, and unworthy. Although my friend tried to tell me about Frankie, I wouldn't listen. I cried and walked away like a dog with her tail between its legs. I didn't listen to my friend, my mother, or even the whispers in my head that proclaimed, I was better than this and created for so much more. The whispers made me feel guilty, and bad about myself, but it was God's vocal expressions, drawing me towards him.

NEW LIFE BEGINS

After my horrific experience with Frankie, I received an invite to a Pentecostal Church, where I sat in the back row. I already felt out of place, so sitting in the back row was safe, no one would notice me. Little did I know it was not about the people noticing me, it was about God seeing my heart. I fell in love with Jesus that day (Oct. 31, 1983), and I have never looked back. I was home in the arms of God. His were the whispers I heard when I was deep in sin with Frankie. He was the one telling me that I was created for so much more. That day, Oct. 31st. 1983, I became "born again." I gave my whole heart to Jesus Christ, and all my sins were washed away by His blood, and I had a new identity. God called me home, gave me a new identity, set me free from sin, shame, the guilt of murder, and every sin that I ever committed!

MOVING FORWARD

Webster defines motion as "the action or process of moving or of changing place or position, the manner of moving the body in walking, stepping, or running." Realizing the pain of my past experiences were not only to draw me to God but were to be used to help others. For 17 years, I have dedicated my life to leading youth ministry by helping teens see themselves through God's lenses. My painful experiences have moved me into becoming a rape crisis counselor, hospice companion volunteer, and bible study teacher to women incarcerated.

Understandingly, it is impossible to fathom how God could undoubtedly use my painful past for good. Still, I fully understand there was a perfect reason why God allowed me to experience such a painful history. I came to believe through my horrific experiences that God is a compassionate God, who never abandoned me. He was always there, even when I tried to commit suicide. In fact, during my distasteful lifestyle, I continued hearing God's whispers, telling me, "I can do better; I was born for so much more." With this in mind, I received a bachelor's in business management, and later a master's in theology. I also obtained a perspective on missions certificate, a competent toast masters certificate, and a few others. I married and raised two beautiful, successful children.

I now train individuals on how to become companions for hospice patients, provide advocacy for rape survivors, encouragement for the incarcerated, and teach high school bible study. Many years later, I realized the attack on my life had much more to do with what I would become in the future, *a warrior for Christ*! God has a lot to offer, which is why I listened to His voice, slowly crawling out of the bed where I was sleeping with the enemy and ran into the arms of His Son, Jesus Christ.

DEBORAH PATTYNAMA:
A LADY OF PURPOSE

A little girl born to become a Lady of Purpose. My name is Deborah Pattynama, and I am a 62-year-old widow. I have been molested and was married to an apostle who suffered from schizophrenia. *But this is not my sad story.* It is my testimony to help set the captives free and clear the fields to help others be set free so that they can walk deeper into the destiny that God has called them into. *Amen.* So, this is my story.

I'm a little girl whose uncle molested her at four years old. I went to my uncle as an adult, looked him in his eyes and told him, "I remember what you did, and I forgive you." He had a tear in his eye. I hugged him and walked away. After many years, my uncle was diagnosed with cancer and the doctor said he was going to die. It's 2019 now, so, I go to him with my husband to remind him that God has forgiven him and to also tell him he will not die of cancer.

My uncle did die, but not of cancer. He died of a heart attack. He passed on, knowing that God and I forgave him. *Amen.*

Let's go back to high school.

I got married straight out of high school on August 28, 1976, I met my husband in church, and we were married for 15 years. I couldn't have any babies for five years, and in that time, I had five miscarriages. *Yes*, I was mad at God, but God is so faithful. After five years, God heard our cry. I had my very own baby *a daughter*, and nine months later, I had a son. In other words, I got a double portion (two babies) in one year, one in January and one in December.

My husband and I were always in church with our family. All of a sudden, we just stopped going to church. In the year 1991, heck broke out. My husband came home one night and said he was moving out, out of nowhere. I didn't cry, I really thought it was a dream. I got up and helped him pack, he walked out of our apartment, and then, I sat on the edge of the bed, asking myself what just happened. He got his own apartment and moved in with another lady.

A week later, I get a call at 2 am asking if Daniel Hernandez lived here. I said he did but he just moved out. They said it was San Antonio Hospital in Upland. I needed to identify Daniel's body, he had passed. I asked about who he was with and what they looked like, they said it was his sister and they described her to me. "Wow," I said. Lord, from a separation to me being a divorcee, now, it's a finale, I'm a widow. The neighbor came to stay with my daughter and son. I drove myself to the hospital, walked in to identify his body. There was my husband, dead blue, with a tube coming out of his mouth. *Jesus, I'm now a widow. How do I tell my children their daddy is dead*? We had an amazing marriage. He was a giver who asked for so little. *It takes two to destroy a marriage and three to make one*. We walked away from God and the enemy was allowed to step in. I drove myself home, traumatized. As I drove, I saw his blue face in every direction I looked. This went on for days.

On the day of his funeral in July 1991, instead of some of his family having compassion, they called me the black widow and other ugly things, I decided to take my daughter and son home. They didn't need to hear such things that were being said. His body hadn't even been put into the earth before we went home. The children had gathered some flowers, once we got home, they had gone door to door telling people their daddy had just died if they would like to buy some of his flowers. My son would sit in his daddy's truck and talk to him. My children lost their daddy at ten and nine years old, myself, a widow at 34.

After becoming a widow, I felt I was missing something in the world. I stopped going to church and stepped into the world without God. He never let me go, yet I let my precious Jesus go. I never got into drugs and drinking but I jumped from relationship to relationship looking just to be loved. I took my children through so much, not being the mother they needed. I got involved with a guy who had an issue with drugs, and I was naïve. People told me he was on drugs, and I never saw them, but sure enough, he was on drugs. He was stealing from me and my children and abused me. I left after years, but I continued to jump from relationship to relationship.

I got remarried to an ex-drill Sergeant, who thought I was one of his little Marines. He was very abusive to me and his 13-year-old daughter. One day she took me into the garage (before I married him) to tell me that her dad was going to hurt me.

I came home early one day. He didn't like that. He then asked me what I was doing at home, and that I had no right to be home when he wasn't home. That day, he picked me up like a football and threw me across the kitchen. I immediately called for my daughter and we both ran into the car in the garage, he somehow stopped the garage door from opening.

After a few minutes that felt like hours, the garage door finally opened. I was able to get the car out of the garage into the driveway where neighbors could hear me screaming. He opened the car door and sat on top of me, he then calls his best friend and said to him, "Listen to b*llsh*t, screaming saying I abused her," while laughing. By then, someone had called the police. They came as he was still sitting on me, they asked him to get off me and he lied to them that he was trying to calm me down, that he doesn't understand why I was crying. Then they made him come sit on the curb in front of the house, and they questioned both of us and my 8-year-old daughter. Finally, they ended up saying that there was no reason to arrest him. *How can I be abused by a man who I married two months ago?*

But I remembered something he told me one day, he said women are so stupid that they don't know that if someone abuses them, they can make a *citizen's arrest.* So, that's exactly what I did. When the police officers took him to jail, that gave me time to gather some of my things and leave, I never went back. Meanwhile, when we got married, he said I should sell my house because we didn't need two, so, I did as he instructed and put all the money from the house into his bank account, and I had no access to the account. So, when I left, I had no money, but I had the precious life of my daughter and myself. His daughter begged and cried that I take her with me, "I'm next, he's going to hurt me," she said. My heart was broken, but I couldn't take her. At 13, she took her dad to court and disowned him as a father.

No one knew where I was for about two months, I felt like such a failure. I was only married two months, not even all our wedding gifts were opened. I started working as a nanny at this time and was permitted to stay with them. The mom asked me if I knew what she did for a living, I said no. "I'm a domestic violence counselor," she said. I knew she was a counselor, but I didn't know what kind. *Wow, God placed me in a place where I would be helped.*

After a month or two, a guy-friend called. We were very close he would do anything for me. He knew in his gut that I had been abused, he asked what happened and where I was staying. Meanwhile, his best friend had just passed away, so, he said, "Come stay with me, the baby (my daughter) can't be bouncing around place to place." I said okay. I had always felt safe with him, so, I moved in with him, he took good care of us always made sure when he got paid, to put a $100 into a special box in case baby needed anything. I never touched that money. One day, I heard the Holy Spirit whisper in my ear, "You need to make a choice, it's either God or him because you're making this man your God." That very day, I called my son and his friend to get a U-Haul and move me. I did it at night when he was at work, I couldn't bear to see his face and hurt him. I moved in with my oldest daughter, then with my brother, and life went on.

I got remarried to an Apostle who suffered from schizophrenia. I didn't know this at the time I married him. After two weeks of marriage, he disappeared. I didn't understand this illness and was frightened by this spirit. It seemed everywhere I went, people with this spirit were attracted to me.

I stayed in my marriage for one year, praying for healing, deliverance for this man and I was full of peace. Then after one year, still as he was gone, I told God I wanted to be released. I then got a divorce.

After that, I got my own apartment. It was just my daughter and I we went forward in life. I then had to have surgery. My son came to stay with me, he took care of my daughter and me. Then I met this guy, we dated, then he said my daughter and I should move in with him. I moved us in with him. Long story short, he began drinking and verbally abusing my daughter. We moved out and went to go live with my dad and mom, and life went on again.

My daughter became pregnant in high school. I told her we will heal and mend together. I dedicated my life to go through the Journey with her. I didn't date for four years. She delivered my grandson, and we were so blessed. Our little miracle. Flat line at birth, but God chose to breathe life into him. Every week he would come to stay with me. The four years I wasn't dating, God began to heal me, deliver me, and set me free. Little did I know he was getting me ready to be a wife, not just a wife but the wife of a man in ministry who was broken just like me. I was done with relationships. I had been through too much. I had been molested, a widow, abused, and married an apostle and he was mentally ill so yes, I was done. BUT GOD SAID IT'S NOT OVER UNTIL HE SAYS IT'S OVER, AMEN. So, this is my JOURNEY AS A LADY WITH A PURPOSE.

So, this man Danny Pattynama (my now husband) messaged me on Facebook, he said "Hi, Deborah how are you?"

I replied, "Fine."

He then asked, "How is your son, Daniel?"

I asked, "Do I know you?"

He said, "Are you Deborah, from New Song Church?"

I said, "No," and he said, "Oh, wrong Deborah."

Little did we both know I was the right Deborah. As we were communicating on Messenger, I had already told him what church I attended, he also knew some people I knew. Of course, I asked questions about him and they said with excitement in their voice, "Oh girl, he's an amazing guy and worship Leader." I still said no within me because I loved my life with the Lord, how far I had come and just the endless time I could pour into my children and grandchildren. God was healing all of us.

On a fateful Sunday, I went to church, and I saw this green SUV Toyota. In my gut I said, *no Lord he's here I didn't invite him, he just showed up*. I walked to the main entrance to the church, there he was standing, waiting for me. I'll never forget his first words he said, "Hey, you," looking me straight in my eyes. In my brain, I was screaming, *NO LORD I CAN'T DO THIS AGAIN!* I didn't want him to sit by me or even breathe the same oxygen I breathe and of course, he sat by me.

Then, my grandson's dad whispered in my ear, "Mom, you're going to marry him." I told him I didn't even know him this was the first time I ever saw him. He repeated it again that I was going to marry him. That was a prophecy, and I didn't even know it. It was hard for my husband to trust me. God showed me visions of different things he had been through, I shared them with him. The first date he took me on was a family gathering. When I got home, my roommate asked me where he took me to, and I told her. She said, "Deborah, he's planning on keeping you." Everywhere we went, they called me his wife.

His worship music was the sound of heaven coming to earth. I would always begin to weep every time he picked up his guitar, I was being healed through his sound to the Lord. My husband asked one day, "What do you want with me? I have nothing to offer you, no job. I live with my sister."

I replied, "when you pick up your guitar and begin to worship, that's more than a million dollars. I receive healing when you play your guitar and that is the most beautiful gift to me." We dated for a year, our Apostle, my spiritual mamma, both came to us at different times and said it was time to get married. We got married on 12/13/14. Our first two years of marriage were difficult. We both had been so broken, but God's first words to me about my husband even before I knew I was going to marry him was: "Deborah, I'm entrusting you with Danny, have his back and bring him water." Even at the time when I was fearful and wanted to leave, I would hear those words. My husband had been hurt deeply by his dad and had a trust issue with him, so, that carried into our marriage. I felt ugly, fat, stupid, and even suicidal. I would get night tormenting spirits that would come to me and tell me, "You will not rest until you kill yourself." I would ask the Lord what was wrong with me.

I'm in ministry, I would go to church, ask for prayers, and the people would say, "okay, I'll keep you in prayer." I was in spiritual trouble, no one saw my tears, and no one took me in their arms and prayed life into me. I WAS IN SPIRITUAL TROUBLE. One day, I messaged a friend I had on Facebook to pray for me, I told her how I felt. She then told me that she was drinking her coffee and the Holy Spirit showed me to her. She came with her husband from having nothing. They kicked and scratched to come to bring us life through the Holy Spirit and help set us free. This did not all happen in one day, they kept coming, praying, and encouraging us.

We now have been married almost six years. Yup, we still go through stuff, but that's life. You take the hand of God, and you forgive over and over. *How great is our God.* We now have worship in our home, we flag together as a husband, wife, and team, sometimes, even as a family with our grandsons and daughter. My husband is part of the worship team at church, and I flag I'M A LADY OF PURPOSE. For God has chosen me out of millions of women to be called the armor-bearer wife of my husband, picking up my weapon, clearing the field to help get him deeper into the destiny that God has called them into. I'm a private professional nanny, I have been a nanny for over 35 years, and I am a mother of many nations. As I help raise babies, I get to plant the seed of Jesus into newborn babies. I stay with one family for four years, sometimes, longer. So, ladies, as you read my testimony, I'm declaring over each and every one of you HEALING.

You are beautiful, despite so vulnerable. You are made in the precious image of the highest, King Jesus. You are royalty. I bless you.

Be encouraged, Amen.

RENEE HASTY:
MY LIFE STORY

In April of 2013, I noticed some itching on my right breast towards the middle of my chest. I ignored the itching thinking it was an insect bite or an allergic reaction to my lotion or body wash. The itching continued, and I continued to ignore it. I decided approximately a month after the itching to Google the words, "breast itch" just out of curiosity. To my shock, there were several articles pertaining to breast itching, and each article made reference to breast cancer. I sat staring at my computer screen in tears. I did not want to immediately think the worst, but I knew I could no longer ignore the signals my body was giving me. I made an appointment with my doctor, and she examined me. The first thing she noticed during my breast exam was a lump I had not felt. I remember that day in her office as if it were yesterday. She said, "Renee there's a noticeable lump in your breast, I need you to have a biopsy today."

"Biopsy?" I asked. "I can't today, I have to go to work this morning." I was scared and making up excuses not to undergo the biopsy. Then, I thought about all the articles referencing breast cancer in my Google search and I agreed to the biopsy. Before the biopsy, I had a mammogram, then waited an additional thirty minutes for the biopsy. The needle for the biopsy was so long I had to turn my head and clench my fists. I was very nervous because it wasn't my first time having a lump in my breast. The first time was when I was in junior high school, and I was playing basketball during PE class. I threw the basketball up for the shot and when my arms extended, the worst pain went through my left breast. My grandparents were called to take me home and to the doctor. I was examined, and the lump was only a cyst it didn't require surgery or treatment. I finally had that lump removed in my early twenties only because it felt weird to me. It moved around when I exercised, the lump was benign. This was on a different breast and the internet research I had done had frightened me.

After the biopsy, the nurse told me the doctor would contact me in a few days with the results. Well, the results were out the very next day. I received a call at work from a different doctor, a male doctor. I remember his call…it was so cold. He said, "Hi, is this Renee?"

I replied, "Yes, this is Renee."

He said, "Are you sitting down? I have your biopsy results."

I said, "No, I'm not sitting down, give me a minute to get where I can speak freely."

"Renee, you have breast cancer," he said so plainly, as if it were no big deal. I screamed at the top of my lungs and ran out of the room. I was screaming through my whole workplace.

All I remember is telling him "I can't, I just can't talk anymore to you," and I hung up. I ran to one of the manager's offices and asked if I could speak with her privately. I told her and she was shocked, and she consoled me. After the next few weeks, my doctors and I planned out a course of action. I was told it was stage three and my options were to remove the lump only, remove my right breast only, or a double mastectomy followed by chemotherapy. The doctor said if we remove the lump, or remove one breast, it could move to my other breast. After thinking, crying, telling my mom, and my three daughters all of my options, I decided to undergo the double mastectomy.

Before my surgery, the doctors had me take two more biopsies of the same breast, although I was scheduled to have both breasts removed the next month. At that time, I didn't understand why, and I was so scared, I didn't ask why I was having additional biopsies. Again, I was scared, very scared, but I decided to begin leaning on the Lord for strength. I took Jesus into every appointment and with each painful procedure, I imagined him holding my hand. I closed my eyes and knew he was there. I could feel his presence.

Before I started to really lean on Jesus, I was praying for him to please heal me and then I won't continue praying for healing, instead, I'll pray for God's will to be done, not my will but His. I changed my prayer because we all want healing for ourselves and our loved ones. Most of us don't want to die from a disease or see our loved ones die. But I thought, *what if I wasn't supposed to live? What if I wasn't supposed to be healed*? I started wanting whatever God wanted for my life, whether it was to leave this earth to be in His kingdom, or to continue my life here. I still want whatever God's will is for me in all that I do. I am so grateful to God I'm still here and as of this month, it will be seven years since God healed my body totally of cancer. Not remission, I am cancer-free, *there is a difference*. I do not take medication. I only have yearly mammograms. I give all praises and honor to God.

GUESS what, Satan literally is attacking my cell phone as I type this email. The words I'm typing keep changing to strange things I didn't type. Satan doesn't want my story to be heard. *Well, Satan you have no place in my life! God is in control, and he is with me.*

NIKKI RENDER:
PEACE AND CHAOS

In the midst of chaos, you don't know what it's like to have peace. The chaos becomes comforting, and you expect and look forward to the insanity. We must recognize the difference between chaos and peace.

Growing up in South Central LA, in an area called *The Jungles*, this was home for me. That's all I knew. I felt a sense of family all around me despite who they were, gang bangers, drug dealers, and violent offenders.

When the sun went down inside the many apartments we lived in, the chaos continued: alcoholism, drug addiction, molestation, teenage pregnancy, adult men preying on young girls for relationships, etc.

My best friend and I made a pact at 14 years old: "Let's get pregnant, be on the county, share a two-bedroom on Section 8, and have our gang banger boyfriends live with us." This was all we saw.

Something changed in me when I saw life outside of my neighborhood. I went to a good junior high school and saw kids whose dreams were very different from mine.

I don't have many good childhood memories or ever feeling loved from those that should have loved me. I can say one of the best things my mother ever did for me was sending me to this school instead of Audubon Junior High, the neighborhood school which is where I should have been. My pact with my friend changed to a pact I made with myself.

I felt God hovering over me at the age of 16. I can remember talking to him, praying, and feeling his presence; feeling secure no matter what I was going through. It is only because of him I survived growing up without losing my mind, having a police record, or addicted to something.

School was always my outlet from the chaos at home. I graduated from high school with top honors and went on to Cal State Long Beach to study nursing. But at 17, I was pregnant.

I vowed to go to college, and never saw my son as a setback. He went to college with me. I was blessed to have free childcare on campus. My son's father is now my husband of 20 years with 30 years being together. We grew up together, weathered the chaos together, and managed to rise above it all.

I am now a nursing professor with my Doctorate Degree. I always share my story with my students to encourage them and let them know anything is possible.

At some point, we must realize that no matter what chaos we grew up in, it does not define who we will become. *Our past is our testimony so that we can help bring peace to others.*

VANESSA BELD:
A LIFE OF FORGIVENESS

F orgiveness is so important to our everyday life. When you forgive, you free yourself. When you hold on to hurt from the other person or persons, it only hurts you because you are not free. You have just put yourself in bondage. You are now enslaved to the hurt and the unforgiveness, and its poisoned and polluted your spirit. Sometimes, you think or even feel that it's hard to forgive a person when he/she has tried to take your life or someone else's. When you think about it, you get this sick feeling in the bottom of your stomach.

At the age of 15, I got pregnant by a man who was 13 years older than me. Shortly after my sixteenth birthday, I was made to get married to him. Before we had our first child, I was afraid of him because he would beat me. I learned to hate him with an undying hatred. What I mean by an undying hatred was that no matter how much love he tried to show me or give me, I hated him to the point that if he had died from anything I would not have cared because I would be free. I found it hard to forgive someone who kicked the life out of me. *Yes*, that's what I said when someone kicks you so hard in your stomach and cause you to lose what could have been a blessing in your life. I had to forgive from a hard place, this would have been my second child.

After four years and two living children later, I divorced him. Many years later, I was walking from one of my cousin's houses. It was on a Saturday afternoon. I accidentally met him in the middle of the street, he saw me and called me by my name. He asked me if I still go to church. I said yes and asked why? That's when he told me that I could not serve God with all the animosity and hatred in my heart. That made me so mad I really wanted to ask him, who is he to say something like that to me? At that point, I didn't even want to be around him. So, I left him standing in the middle of the street as I walked away. I was so mad, I could feel my blood getting hot and my eyes started burning and turning red, then tears started running down my face. Because all those feelings came back to create fear and I was scared that he might hit me again. I had to at that moment, deal with all my emotions. You know he was right. However, he was the one who made me feel the way I did about him.

I spoke to one of the missionaries in the church about what he said. She said, "While I know you don't want to hear this, but he is right. You can't serve God with all that hatred in you," and she continued "to be honest with you, He's not hearing your prayers." These words of hers made me mad. Although both were right, I was not ready to accept what was been said to me. I felt I had every right to hold to my feelings, after all he was the one who put them there.

Many years went by before I decided to deal with my issue within myself. Inside, I felt like I was a slow pressure cooker ready to explode but I didn't want to take my rage out on anyone, *just him*. But I was too afraid to do anything about it, so I carried these feeling around with me like a hidden suitcase inside of me and I was the only one who knew about it and what was inside of that suite for many years. You see, everything I was carrying inside of me was everything God asked we get rid of from the **NLT Ephesians 4:31: Get rid of all bitterness, rage, anger, harsh words, and slander, as well as all types of evil behavior.**

At that point in my life, I could not bring myself to grips of getting rid of anything that God told me to get rid of because I was in a deep prison, and it was so dark. I withdrew myself from a lot of church people and family. The crazy thing about the prison I was in was that I felt the need to go to church, hoping to hear one word. A word that would free me from my own self-made prison. My desire was strong, I felt if I missed going to church, God would not free me.

Let me tell you this one thing, I was free all the time, but I did not know how to walk in my freedom. I kept repenting for the same thing over and over again. God freed me the first time I asked him to free me, but I did not accept that I had to work for forgiveness. The one thing I did not do was let it go from my heart. The day I let all that stuff leave from my heart, I have never felt so *free* and had so much peace. Forgiving that person freed me, I am not in bondage at all, and I am free. Why? Because God made me free. *It's true.* **NLT John 8:36 So if the son set you free, you will indeed be free.** It is also true if you confess your faults. **NLT James 5:16 confess your sins to each other and pray for each other so that you may be healed. The earnest prayer of a righteous person has great power and produces wonderful results.**

My result is that *I am free*. Because I learned how powerful forgiveness really is, I forgave. I know the pain is real and sometimes, the events replay in your mind and your heart skips many beats. Acknowledge every pain, hurt, frustration, all the sadness, even when you get mad because you feel that you allowed this to happen to you once or even again. Acknowledge all this, now, surrender it to God. It's time for you to be free in your heart, mind, spirit, and soul.

RENA NEAL

I was a single mom raising four beautiful children. A long time ago, I made the decision to be by myself. No boyfriend, nothing. At that time, it was the best decision I had made in years. Times were hard for us, but times could also be great. I worked various temporary jobs. When you are a single parent with four children, jobs just didn't understand that when they are sick, you have to be at home with them. I spent many nights alone, sitting up, looking at my children wondering how I was going to make it. Wondering if the decision to be by myself was the best decision for me and for them. I would be so depressed. I would go days without sleeping. I would sit there staring at them laying quietly in my bed. They all loved to crawl in my bed at night and sleep. I would end up leaving my room sometimes because I couldn't sleep with four bodies in my bed. I loved my children and wanted the best for them but sometimes, I would wonder if I was the best for them.

Was there another way for them to have a better life? I would think about who in my family or their father's family would love and take care of them as I did. If I left this world, who would worry about them, defend them, and let them know that they are some great human beings? It was sad because I could think of no one. My relationship with my family was strained at that time. I did not communicate with them much. Their father was not the best person, and his family was not the best example of a loving family that I would feel at peace leaving them with.

I wanted my pain to end. I wanted to end everything. I tried to go to church at times, I tried to pray, I tried to read my bible. I was seeking peace and comfort and I didn't know where it would come from. I had great friends. I had a wonderful "godmother" who was there when I needed her, but that was not enough for me at that time. I needed something more. I desired to have someone love me in return, give me the confidence I desperately needed, and I didn't know where it would come from. I needed someone to take away my loneliness, to heal my broken heart.

This one night, sitting in the darkness, feeling the loneliness again, then suddenly I felt an overwhelming sense of peace. In my spirit, God was saying I should keep going. He said I was going to be okay. No one knew my pain. No one knew my loneliness, my finances, my doubt. No one knew that I wanted to end it. *To give up*. But God did. He met me at the lowest point. He stayed with me in my spirit. He gave me encouragement.

The Bible says in **Daniel 10:19, that God will give you a "suddenly" moment.** God spoke to me in my spirit that night and He met me at my loneliest and darkest moment. I made it through that night and many more nights. God gave me the peace and comfort I needed. I have learned that God had plans for me. I knew he wanted me to keep going because I knew he would never leave me.

Many years passed by, and it took a while for me to join a church. I was still seeking Him and I knew where I could find Him. I have come a long way from then. My children are adults and I have lost two of my sons. No one can know the heartache a mother carries when there is a loss of two children, but God never forsook me. He was right there when I needed him. He did not forsake me.

I hope this will help someone who may be struggling as a single parent like me. I want you to know that the *Joy of the Lord will always give you strength*. Life has had its challenges, but the battle was never mine alone. Keep going, keep praying, keep believing. God will meet you just as he met me.

MONA TURNER HAWKINS:
THIS IS MY STORY

I was born and raised in South Central Los Angeles, in a two-parent household with eight siblings, and attended school all within LAUSD. Life as I knew it was good up until I graduated high school and was faced with my own decisions to either attend college or work. I chose to work. I worked as a full-time bank teller. After working for ten months, I decided that if I wanted to get promoted with other opportunities, I needed to attend college and obtain a degree. I stopped working and attended a local university. Having no income, parents could not afford my bills I had accumulated, and I did not want my boyfriend taking care of me. What am I to do?

Well, my boyfriend offered and I accepted. I was married at 22 years old, *young*. I am lucky. I am still married, now 34 years. I am not in my marriage because I have to be – I am married because I *choose* to be. I write this story because so often we hear of women who stayed in marriages for the kids or the house. I say NEVER risk your happiness for the sake of others. *Be your own happy.* Never worry about what others think of you, be you! Today, because of my perseverance, after raising three sons (a set of twins), all have graduated from college, I am a doctoral student attending Pepperdine University.

JESSICA EVERETT:
MY PAIN…MY PERSEVERANCE

A s far back as I can remember, I knew I was destined for something great. I was always fantasizing about my future being filled with magic and greatness, knowing deep down that I was something special. As I look back to my childhood as an adult, I now realize I've always had a purpose. Through all the trials and tribulations since then, I know I have always been protected. During some of my darkest days, I would question my faith, or wonder *why me.* I see now that my purpose was to help others, share my story, and give others strength. This is the greatness that I always knew I was destined for.

When I was a child, I watched my parents divorce at a very young age but never understood the effects at that time. I think back now and realize, this was my first experience with loss and gratitude at the same time because my mom was exceptional, and I can't remember a time without her by my side. As the years went on, my mom remarried, and we instantly had a larger family (my stepdad and his children). We moved to a new town and began our life as a unit. We traveled on weekends, played games, spent quality time, and welcomed two more siblings to our now six-child home. Obviously, there are still ups and downs with such a large family but one thing that never wavered was our love for family and our commitment to each other.

As years went on, I was now growing into my teenage years, active in dance classes and an avid soccer player. I participated in the D.A.R.E. program and was a straight-A student. I had very high expectations of myself because I was aware of my capabilities.

At the age of thirteen, everything changed. I was molested by my dance instructor. The shame that comes behind something so horrible takes away the anger you would normally feel, and this is because you start to wonder what you did wrong, how you could have prevented it, and the truth is at thirteen years old, how would you?

It has taken my entire life until recently to realize that it was never my fault. I was a child, and a child does not possess the coping mechanism or tools to prepare you for something so terrible. I think from this experience and growth as a woman, sharing may in turn help another child or woman to overcome the blame and shame that they feel. Because of this experience and being so young without the tools to help get me through my personal sadness, I turned to drugs.

I was thirteen when I first tried methamphetamine. It was in my middle school bathroom with one of my friends and I was blown away at how it made me feel. I remember that I was still so high after school, I had to smoke marijuana to try and bring my high down before I went home. I was so nervous that my mom would know but I made it through that first night. From there everything went downhill. I was not using every day, but my behavior was changing, my grades were slipping, I was no longer interested in sports or dance. I was like a ticking time bomb as some would say. I was eventually kicked out of school for the entirety of that school year, and it was during this time my parents sent me to a boarding school in Boston. While in Boston, I was not using methamphetamine anymore, but I was smoking marijuana almost daily, and not knowing until years later. This was my mind telling me that one drug was better than another, and it wasn't so bad. As long as I didn't do methamphetamines, I was okay. *It's a baffling disease to say the least*. Even though I still managed to be a straight-A student once again, I have always loved school.

A few years later, coming home for holidays and summers was not enough, I wanted to be home again for good, so I masterminded a way to get kicked out and return to California.

I was sixteen at the time and I wanted to be back with my friends. When I came home, I had too many credits for the high school I enrolled in, so I ended up graduating at the age of sixteen, top five in the state of California, and was accepted into a couple of great colleges. Even though I was an exceptional student, I was very young and was not ready for a university, so I came back home and went to a community college. It was during this time I was using again, not only marijuana and methamphetamine but drinking as well. I was not only the life of the party, but I also became a supplier for many different drugs. I came into a dark lifestyle that had many dangerous consequences. Time went on and I wasn't changing, I was a disappointment to my family and myself. I knew they loved me, but this was not the life they expected from me, and with all the shame and guilt built on to what I already experienced, I kept swirling down the rabbit hole.

When I was twenty, I met the father of my first two children. We were both active in addiction and making a lot of money selling drugs. Not even a year into the relationship he became extremely violent and was physically, mentally, and emotionally abusive. Not far after the abuse began, I became pregnant with my son. During the entire pregnancy, I was abused on a daily basis. The abuse became so bad I wouldn't be able to leave the house because of the bruises all over my body. Once again, I was ashamed, scared, sad, and now angry. Once my son was born, the abuse did not stop. There would be days I would be choked unconscious, and he would catch my son out of my arms as I fell to the ground. I was kicked, hit, spat on, anything you can think of it happened. So many people ask me now why didn't I leave. *How could I?*

I had separated myself from my support because of my addiction. They did not accept my lifestyle and I was so ashamed to face them even though they loved me so much. What was I supposed to do? I again did not have the proper tools to remove myself from this situation. Then, I became pregnant again with my daughter. It was during this pregnancy that God knew I couldn't get away on my own. I believe he prepared me for an exit. I was three months pregnant when he beat me so badly, I had to be hospitalized. He was arrested, and this was my escape. My family helped me remove my things and I was free. I do have to admit that I felt an obligation, *to this day I do not know why*, to visit him in jail. After a short period of time that went away, I was a single mom, with two babies, and I met my husband.

I tell myself now that this is a fairytale ending, but in the beginning, not so much. I was still active in my addiction and living a lifestyle not intended. I was in and out of jail on felony charges and had a scarce relationship with my family. I became pregnant with our baby girl and welcomed her into this world in 2010. Six months later, my husband went to prison for the next five years. I was alone now with three children. Through everything, what mattered to me the most was being a mom, and God not only removed me from a toxic relationship, but he was also preparing me for my rock bottom.

On October 10, 2012, my life changed forever, I was arrested again and left my kids with a friend. During the eleven days I spent in jail, my kids were picked up from my friend's house by CPS. This was my rock bottom, my kids meant more to me than anything and there was no going back at this point. I remember the day I was released, I hit the ground running.

It took me less than six months to regain custody of my children, all while going to school, working a program, working part-time, and staying clean.

I am celebrating eight years of sobriety this year, just graduated college, married with a beautiful home, and working full-time, third generation in my family's company. I have my family back, my life back. My husband is an exceptional man, who has been through hell and back with me. For that, I will forever be grateful. My children too have seen some sad days, but they are amazing human beings as well.

When I say God is good, I mean God is GREAT. I have looked death in the face many times and I am still here because *I do have a purpose. I always did.* I do not live with shame, I live in gratitude, humility, and love.

My values are true, and I feel blessed, as my experiences have helped me evolve into who I was destined to be.

There are so many in-betweens throughout my journey, but my hope is that by sharing these small details, someone will understand that even in the depths of despair, there is light. With commitment and accountability, strength, and perseverance, you can succeed. You are not a survivor – you are a warrior!

CHARLENE J. ANDERS: FINDING MY VOICE

I was born August 3, 1960, in a small little town I did not know existed: Kern County Bakersfield. I was born to Carol Luvenia (Lindsey) Fowler and William Lee Fowler Sr. They were young parents at only 15 and 18, respectively. I was the oldest of four siblings. I grew up with a step-grandmother and grandfather on my mother's side and a grandmother on my father's side. I was incredibly young when my dad's father died. There is only one snapshot memory I have of him, and it is embedded in fond memory.

Like most young parents who have experienced traumas in their lives, they tend to parent through those traumas. My parents were no different. They both were stuck in the throes of substance abuse. Although my parents were not physically abusive, they were at times neglectful and not present. My mother was a typical "stay at home mom" and my father was a foreman. In one way, we were blessed with the boss he had. Many other men would have been fired from their jobs and not permitted to return. My dad's boss not only would take him back after his binges. He would make sure that as often as my dad wanted to work, he made it available to him.

My love for my parents far outweighed the negative stigma attached to their addictions. The violence that my parents would

106

engage in was both implosive and explosive toward each other. From grade one to about grade four, life was a blur. What I do remember during that time was my fear of coming home simply because I never knew whose blood would be on the walls. I remember many days of being by myself, walking home from Gettysburg Elementary School, looking up into the sky. I am not sure if I was having conversations with God, but I can tell you that it was during one of these walks home that I encountered God for the first time.

Being the oldest automatically assigned me to the responsibility of my younger sibling. For me, it seemed easy to assume the role of caretaker for my younger sibling. I do not remember having a thought of hating my birth order. I just remember that I had to protect them. I would create different activities for us to do. My brother and I were highly creative. I made sure there was always something for us to do. The world was our playground. Now that I look back, I realize some of those activities were extremely dangerous, like jumping fences and jumping off the raised garage door onto a mattress. They say that God protects babies and fools. Well, He certainly protected us.

There are many angles I can take with my life story, but for the sake of time, I would like to follow the vein of my creative development culminating with the writing and publishing of my first mini novel *Living in His Presence, while Abiding in His*. This was a major accomplishment for me. It was the first time I discovered the value of my voice in written form. Let me not get ahead of myself. As a child, I would make up stories about there being a mix up in the hospital when I was born. My stories were so detailed and animated that my younger cousins really believed my biological parents were not mine. For a period, I honestly believed there was a mix up at the hospital. Some might say I was developing an uncanny knack for lying. I saw it as perfecting a creative imagination with the ability to put what I saw in words.

My creative imagination allowed me to survive the periods in time when my parents would engage in aggressive, violent, and at times bloody confrontations with each other. Imagination became my coping mechanism. It was my escape, my refuge. I did not realize it at the time, but the stifling noise of the violence not only created a sense of instability within myself it also conditioned me to keep my voice silent. I equated the raised voices with increased violent actions.

When my mother died, I was 12. I ended up living with my mother's oldest sister for six years. Now, this is another story that carried its own set of challenges that added to my silence. My aunt and uncle were kind to me and my baby sister. We were the only two they took. My brothers stayed in a foster home until the courts gave them back to my dad.

My uncle and aunt were a typical middle-class two-parent household. My uncle worked and my aunt was a stay-at-home mom. I had five cousins. The oldest cousin and I were the same age just a few months apart with me being the oldest. The six years living with them was an internal hell for me. The cousin next to me seemed to have major control over the household. I know this might sound strange, but it was the way I saw my new living situation. Every time she would get mad at me (which was quite often and for most of the time it was just because I was breathing), it felt like the whole house was mad at me and no one would talk to me. So, once again, I resorted to my own world of words and began journaling.

Journaling gave me a way of setting my feelings free. I could yell in writing and not disturb anyone else. I could cry in words, and no one sees my tears and tell me to suck it up. I could even curse them out because of the silent treatment and not get into trouble *or so I thought*. One day, I was walking home from middle school, and I had this sickening feeling in the pit of my stomach. I did not know what it was, I sensed something terrible was about to happen. Sure enough, just as I stepped into my aunt's house I was greeted by a fist to the stomach. Several more blows proceed after that like rapid fire. All I could hear was, "So you want to tell me to f##* off!"

My cousin, the one that I felt controlled the house, had found my diary, and gave it to my aunt. She was angry but never thought for one moment to sit me down and ask me why I wrote the things I did. I felt they had no clue about the kind of environment that my siblings and I grew up in. She had no clue of how much exposure to violence at an early age could make you sink into a shell or cause one to become a rebellious terror. I could not explain, *no, I dare not explain*. I just took the beating. I threw my diary away and vowed never to write another word. I kept that vow from 1974 until 1995.

In 1995, God was ready for me to rediscover my voice in writing. I was standing in church, and I heard these words, "You can never be more committed to him (Pastor) than he (husband) is committed to Him (God)." I then heard, *write*! It was from these words that my storyline for my book came. I started writing for the next decade it seemed. I finished this project in 2012. There it sat, voice to paper. I did not realize how much the trauma of the diary book incident was controlling and keeping me from going any further with my finished work. I was too afraid to let anyone else read my work for fear of judgement.

My literary work was me and I was it. To allow someone else to read it would put me in a vulnerable place of judgement. I was judged and punished for my literary work in my diary. I internalized the course of events that occurred that day in 1974 and the internal vow I made now had a lording position over my freedom to move forward. Until one day, I met this very gentle, kind, and funny woman who was an editor. The ease I felt with her prompted me to blurt out, I wrote a book. Her gleeful response seemed to totally snatch me out of the grips of fear of exposure.

She said, "Oh, do tell me about it."

As I proceeded to share the theme of the story, she gave me her complete undivided attention. She did not just give me her undivided attention, she looked like one who was watching the best movie in the world with a bowl of hot buttered popcorn in her lap.

Ladies With Purpose

She then encouraged me to let her look at the book. She committed to editing the book for a nominal price. I promise you every motion from the time I opened my mouth seemed to be totally guided by a force beyond myself. She not only edited my book, but she also helped me to self-publish it. Her confidence in me, in my storyline, rebirthed my self-confidence. I was reintroduced to my voice in writing. I realized that I had something to say, and it was something of value.

JESSICA BRADLEY: LETTING GO

I was raised a Catholic so, I was always aware of the Lord, but as I got older, I felt a pull to be less in a religion and did not really pursue God for quite a few years. I met my husband in my early twenties and he had recently accepted Jesus as his savior, so he was very much ready to dive into the faith walk and wanted me to join him. Somewhat reluctantly, I started attending non-denominational Christian church with my husband. I still very much had my guard up regarding God. In many ways, I viewed God as cold, angry, and distant, and certainly not wanting a relationship with me directly. The concept of a loving Father seemed lost to me, since my father and I had a rocky relationship growing up.

My life has brought me through many ups and downs. One of the most significant spiritually life changing seasons for me has been between the years of 2015 to 2019. Up to that point, I attended church regularly and served in ministry but in many ways, I always walked with one foot in worldly wisdom and one foot in faith. My husband has always had a very solid faith, and can pray through any obstacle, in fact, this is one of the things I love the most about him. On the outside looking in, it looked like I had everything a woman could want. I finished my second master's degree in psychology in 2016, had the big house in the suburbs, two cars, married, and had a beautiful daughter with a decent job. The issue was that inside of me there was a storm brewing that I could not contain. The Lord was calling me to the deep, and I was not willing or ready to give control up to the Lord, though I desperately needed to.

I had always been the type to set my mind on something and go for it and get it. I would pray about decisions, but oftentimes I'd move forward well before I received a real revelation from God. I had studied psychology throughout my whole education so, I very much believed in conventional healing through changing your thoughts, habits, therapy, etc. I believed in miracles but did not really see them manifest in my own life. My marriage had started to suffer not long after we bought our home because it was much more then we could afford. My husband's income had been reduced, so much of the financial burden rested on me. We had a lot of struggles over control and had fallen into codependency in the relationship. I grew ever more exhausted and bitter at trying to hold everything up financially. On top of this, my daughter was starting to show signs of sensory and learning disabilities and would often meltdown and have behavioral issues.

We started attending a Bible study in 2015 and I decided to get baptized as an adult (I had been christened as a baby). After that moment I noticed a spiritual shift start happening within myself. I love to sing and worship, and I noticed when I sang, there was a different sound that came out and clarity in hearing the Lord's voice. I felt the Lord softening my heart little by little, and my gift of discernment got sharper. I had gone through traditional therapy in order to finish my degree in 2015 and that helped me, but there was a much deeper spiritual root that I could not ignore. After I finished my degree in 2016, I distinctly remember hearing the Lord tell me NOT to pursue my marriage family therapist license. I was totally confused, I thought *this was my whole purpose, Lord, to become a licensed counselor, the reason I sacrificed the last two years.* I had been working on this degree while working full time and often traveling because of work. I put everything I had into it, but at the same time, often felt guilty for neglecting my family with long nights at school. How could the Lord tell me not to move forward?

I continued to work at my job but the storm in me kept brewing. We were serving four days a week at our church at the time, and it felt like I was just going through the motions. There was no joy anymore, just religious duty. My husband and I kept fighting with no resolution, we ended up getting one of our cars repossessed, and I just felt like a complete failure. We had gotten approved for a program to help us keep our home, but I knew it was only a temporary fix. In 2017 I could hear the Lord speaking to me over and over and telling me to *"let it go."* I remember praying over and over about what he meant.

As 2017 progressed, things just kept getting tenser between my husband and I, reaching a breaking point when I was seriously considering divorce. I let my husband know this, and I broke down into a deep depression, something that I had never experienced before. The pain of not moving forward with my career, the marriage and family struggles, coupled with the financial and inner turmoil was way more than I could take. In the midst of this time, I cried out to God in a way I never had before. I prayed with a fervency and asked God what I should do. I heard Him say again, *"let it go."* I ended up leaving my job as I felt this was part of the letting go the Lord was asking of me. This was a sense of security and control. My husband was okay with it, as he knew if the Lord commanded it, things would work out. My daughter was happy to have her mom home more again. For the first time in so many years, I felt a sense of freedom that I had never experienced. A month after I left my job, I attended a church service focused on deliverance and that same night, I received the miracle of the Lord completely removing my depression. I could not believe it! He showed me a tangible miracle, and my entire view of healing and the Lord shifted.

God led me through deeper spiritual healing in 2018 in the form of freedom of prayer and deliverance. My trust in the Lord grew stronger, and I could truly say He is a loving Father in my life. I also learned what it meant to truly rest in the Lord. My husband also went through deliverance and after these healings, our marriage improved significantly. We might still have issues come up, but our responses and ability to communicate are much more productive. We pray together more and recognize the tactics of the enemy sooner. We now get more involved in deliverance and marriage ministries.

In 2019, we were told we would need to short sell our home. Though this hurt, I believe the Lord prepared us for it. We were ready to let it go. What the enemy would have used to destroy us just a few years earlier became a testimony of the faithfulness of God. Sometimes letting go is the biggest act of faith one can ever make. Letting go lets the Lord have room to add what He wants to your life, and you do not have to be the one to carry it all.

Matthew 11:28-30(NIV)

28 - "Come to me, all you who are weary and burdened, and I will give you rest. 29 - Take my yoke upon you and learn from me, for I am gentle and humble in heart, and you will find rest for your souls. 30 - For my yoke is easy and my burden is light."

ERIKA CANADA:
WHERE DO I START?

W here do I start? Is what I asked myself when challenged with the task of sharing a testimony of God's goodness and wondrous works in my life.

God has brought me out of many things. Of course, it always seems like we leave one battle and enter a new one; and so often, we forget about all that He has already done for us and the many challenges He has delivered us from. We're human, so it's normal and God understands, but we can't stay there. God deserves His glory and as we remind ourselves of what He's already done, it encourages us to know He is the same God and will work out our present situation as well.

One of the testimonies I'd like to share is how God delivered me from cancer. It all began with a breast cancer event I attended. As with many of us, when attending something like that, we get nervous and are prompted to get checked (if we hadn't already). It had been over a year since my last mammogram, so I jumped on it and made an appointment. I figured while I was at it, might as well do a well-woman exam, although it wasn't quite time yet. Well, I soon found out, that decision was not by chance. My mammogram came out just fine, however, my pap exam was abnormal. After a series of follow up appointments and an outpatient biopsy, I was diagnosed with stage 1 cervical cancer. At that moment, I felt like the ground was pulled from underneath me. I hadn't brought anyone with me to get the news, because I was certain that all was well. I barely remember getting home that day, everything seemed foggy, and I cried like a baby. Eventually, I pulled myself together with the prayers, support, and encouragement from my family and friends. I had to "be strong" before telling my boys. I didn't want to show fear but instead, show faith and confidence while I talk to them, so they can feel confident that all would be well. I was soon scheduled for a total hysterectomy to assure nothing was missed. My doctors wondered *what made me get checked.* They expressed how "lucky" I was to have caught the tumor at such an early stage. It was so small that the first CT scan missed it. Due to my doctor ordering the cone biopsy, that was how the tumor was actually discovered. We know, that was not by luck or by chance, it was all ordained and led by God. He used that breast cancer event to get me into the doctor's office. Although the doctors spoke positively and encouraging, I still battled with those thoughts of *why me...Why did this happen? I try to take care of myself, practice healthy eating, healthy habits...I love the Lord...so why me?*

Post-surgery was one of the worst weeks I ever physically experienced. I stayed in the hospital an entire week and dealt with the worst pain I had ever experienced. The day after my surgery, I was presented with the unwanted news that they wanted to follow up with radiation and low dose chemotherapy; "just to be sure". They were pretty confident they had taken care of the tumor but didn't want to risk missing something that was too small to detect. I was discouraged and heartbroken to say the least, scared of the side effects, afraid I'd lose my hair or worse. I asked so many questions, I know I drove the doctors crazy. I was soon scheduled to have radiation treatments five days a week, Monday-Friday, and chemo every Wednesday for eight weeks. I felt so discouraged because I thought for sure I'd be done with all this after I recovered from my surgery.

After a few weeks of recovery, the treatments began. Radiation didn't seem so bad; it was about three minutes laying on the radiation bed with this huge machine circling around me. Although it didn't seem bad, I knew that it could cause harm. Every session, I prayed the entire time. Then chemo day came on Wednesday. I packed water, jolly ranchers, and salty snacks to prepare for a full day at the doctor's office. I was scheduled to be in treatment from 9 am to 5 pm. Yes, like a full-time job. I walked into this room filled with cancer patients and felt so many emotions. I felt defeated because I was there and felt hurt seeing so many suffer from this horrible disease. I will never forget what it felt like when that needle was placed in my arm and the chemo drug began to go through my body.

The tears begin to roll because I felt the most horrible sensation entering my bloodstream. I could feel the warmth travel from my arms to my head and throughout my body. *What is this?* I thought to myself, *this can't possibly be low dose!* The researcher that I am, I pulled out my phone and began to Google the name of the drug to compare what low dose was, compared to the dose written on my bag. Wouldn't you know, my dose was indeed higher than what the information I found on Google deemed low dose. I quickly called for my nurse because I was not going to let them give me more than what they said. Well, it was then explained to me that the dosage is calculated based upon the individual's body weight and other factors, not a standard one size fits all dosage. "Oh," I said, once again feeling defeated, because I thought if they made a mistake, surely a lower dose wouldn't feel so terrible. After the first treatment, they told me to start taking my anti-nausea medication right away. This would help once the medicines they fed through my veins wore off and lessen the nausea side effects. I felt weird, a bit nauseous but I did as they said and kept taking the nausea medicine. By late Saturday, I would begin to start feeling better, finally. I would have to enjoy that moment and day of relief because Monday, we would start all over again.

I figured maybe the second week would be a little easier, but when chemo day came around again, I felt just as horrible, if not worse. This time, I cried from Wednesday throughout the weekend because I did not want to do chemo again. I began to feel that I couldn't tolerate it. I asked God for wisdom. I told God in my prayers, "I believe You already healed me and if You're in agreement please fix this and make them stop." I prayed that He would fix it, or that He would guide me and words of my mouth to tell the doctors I was opting to stop the chemo treatments. I even solicited the prayers of my family to stand with me for a miracle. What happened next was nothing short of that.

On Monday, I went in for my routine weekly check and my radiation treatments. On Monday, they'd ask how my weekend went, how did I tolerate the chemo treatment and if I experienced anything abnormal since my last check. I told them I felt bad through Saturday as usual, slight nauseous, and I'd had some ringing in my ear. The nurses wrote everything down and said, "Okay, we will be sure to share with the doctor." I then went on to my Monday radiation treatment and then home. On Tuesday, I went in for my radiation treatment and when I came out and was getting in my car to leave, I heard my chemo doctor's voice yell, "Oh, hey Erika, the girls told me about your ear. No more chemo for you until we get that checked!" I yelled back, "Okay!"

Needless to say, I was in total shock. I got in my car with this puzzled surprised look and said, "No way! God did you really just answer my prayer already?" I didn't want to get ahead of myself, but I felt in my heart that He had! I immediately texted my boys, mom, sister, brother, and sister-in-love to tell them what had just happened. *Could it be?!* Well, the next day was Wednesday...chemo day! I went in for my 9 am appointment and was called into a regular room instead of the chemo room. My doctor said she was sending me to an ear, nose, and throat specialist because the ear ringing was definitely a side effect of that chemo drug, and she was concerned about hearing loss. Well, after a not-so-great visit with the specialist who yelled at me, stating it was too soon to determine. I'd have to choose my life over my hearing, I was sent back to the chemo doctor.

I told her what the specialist said, and she was surprised. That didn't sound like the physician she knew, but it didn't matter. I know now that negative behavior was a distraction to discourage me and make me think my God was not about to deliver me. My chemo doctor went on to tell me that it didn't matter what he said because she and the radiation doctor had already discussed it and decided to cancel further chemo treatments. She stated that it was only for extra precautions and that they believe they took care of the problem in surgery anyway.

They decided they'd only continue with radiation. I didn't have to endure the additional four-six treatments of chemo as planned! Praise be to God! They continued with very brief radiation on my abdomen area for about eight weeks, five days a week. They expected various side effects from that as well, but I stayed in prayer and took care of myself at home to keep my skin and body as strong as possible. When it was over, the doctor was amazed that I didn't experience any of the usual side effects. She stated, "You handled this very well, much better than expected." I had no expected burning of the skin. When I began treatments, I felt in my heart that God was telling me to use aloe vera on my skin every day after treatments. I was not able to use anything on my skin within hours before treatment, so I used it afterward. I believe that is what protected my skin from damage. I also drank lots of water and took healthy multivitamins. Again, all praises be to God! Shortly after, I was back to work and on the road to complete healing.

In the midst of the trial, during my hospital stay, God revealed to me an event that He would have me produce, to bring men and women together to discuss all cancers and the importance of being proactive and keeping up with our routine checkups. He used a woman that volunteered at the hospital, going to certain patients giving them a mini tea party in their hospital room to cheer them up. I happened to be chosen, in spite of me saying "no." It was the day they told me I had to follow-up with chemo and radiation. I wanted to sit alone and feel sorry for myself, so God sent that woman to me that day. She had fresh flowers, vintage linen, a variety of tea sets for me to choose from. I felt like a little girl. I was so excited because these are things I love and no one there would have known that. She set it all up on my bed tray, had me choose the flavor tea I wanted, and even placed a cute little tea cookie on my saucer. We talked, shared, laughed, and cried. By the time she left, we were both uplifted. She told me, "I came here to bless and uplift you, and here you did that for me!" *It was definitely mutual...*I knew it was God because they had no idea I had recently started collecting vintage style teacup sets. The very type she set up for me to use during our little party. Later that day, the woman came back and said God placed it on her heart to give me the teacup set I chose to use during our visit. I'll never forget that day. It was just what I needed to uplift me.

A year later, I produced that tea party event that God revealed to me on my sick bed, and He laid it on my heart to pay it forward by blessing all in attendance with their very own vintage teacup set. No one could believe that I didn't want to charge attendance. I was determined this would be a free event and that I'd find the perfect tea sets to gift my guests, and God provided. We were blessed to have a close family friend who is a gourmet chef, prepare the most amazing authentic English Tea style meal, and heard from several other women who had suffered from various cancers. I feel in my heart and was told by many, that was not intended to be a one-time event. I truly believe my experience was the birthing of something God wants to do through my life. When I told the volunteer from the hospital what she had inspired, she cried and said she had been contemplating if she would continue to volunteer at the hospital. She said after hearing my story, she knew she did have to continue her work as a volunteer. She didn't realize how her obedience had truly affected my life, my journey. We all have a gift and at times, we don't understand why we go through certain things, but we never know how God will use our experiences, our gifts, and our gestures of love toward people. That volunteer's obedience had a huge impact during a very low moment in my life. As a result, my experience can have a huge impact on others as well.

I thank and praise God! It was Him and only Him. Trust me, I didn't go through that time calm, full of faith every single day or without shedding many tears. I admit, it was a very challenging time for me, BUT GOD...I knew (fearfully as I was), where my help would come from and WHO to lean on...and HE brought me through... HE carried me through...HE, our faithful Father God, healed me in the mighty name of Jesus, by His Blood that was shed for ALL of us! Four years later, here I am, completely healed, and forever CANCER FREE! Glory and all thanks be to GOD! He will carry you through any and every challenge you find yourself in. *Trust Him*...cry, pray, cry and pray again...but trust Him!

FIRST LADY LUCY BRYANT: HUMBLE BEGINNINGS

I grew up in Shreveport, Louisiana, not a small town, but definitely not a large one. I'm the oldest of three. My mom was never really a part of our lives, she struggled with alcohol from the time I was born until her death. It is hard as a child to watch your mom go in and out of rehab. I loved her so much, and like most kids, I believe my parents are invincible. As a kid, when she was clean, she was the best mom to exist. However, when she would go back to her old surroundings, she would fall into the same trap that got her there. I watched this for years, it caused me to be very shy and withdrawn. The lack of her love caused me to want to feel that unconditional love you're supposed to feel from your parents.

At the age of seven, I had my first experience of the absence of my mom's teachings. A neighbor, who was probably 65, would watch us for my uncle. He would tell me to sit on his lap and he would stick his tongue in my mouth and rub me. I became numb from my mommy not being around, and a dad who I barely knew. I had several other experiences like that one, one even coming from my sister's father, but none of those things define me any longer. I have so many experiences of abuse in my family.

At the age of 19, I left Louisiana for California only having one relative there. I knew I could no longer survive here. By faith, I walked alone, not knowing God was with me the whole time. In California, my defining moment was when I meet my children's father. It would be a roller coaster of drugs and alcohol that would be a defeat for him but triumph for me. I found God through his own personal search for God.

He went to a small apostolic church, and I soon joined. It was life-changing. I experienced God on a whole other level. I was transformed into a beautiful butterfly, instantly I knew my worth, I knew my value. No longer would I be bound to anything or anyone. In walking away from my kids' dad. I was by myself, but never alone. Every step of the way he guided me, he taught me with his own hand how to love my children, how to provide, how to train them in the things of God.

Early on, God told me I would marry a pastor. I had to kiss a lot of frogs to get to him, but he found me bruised but not broken, and he loved me enough to call me his own.

BIRTEAL SCHELLS:
NO COMPROMISE

I was twenty-one years old and in college during the fall quarter, taking prerequisite classes to qualify for the nursing program. I worked on campus, had my own car, and aside from living at home with my parents, was fairly independent. But that is not what this story is about. This story is about how I almost compromised.

Growing up in a Christian home and attending church conferences and teen conventions, one of the things I heard was, "Don't be unevenly yoked." *What does that really mean?* My understanding at that time was that if I, a Christian girl, wanted a boyfriend, he also had to be a Christian. *Simple, right?* Not hard. At that time, anyone could say they were a Christian but live a life that was not Christ-like.

When approached by guys, one of the things I would ask to filter them out was, "Do you go to church?" If they answered yes, then that was a plus. Next would be a list of intrusive questions such as, what church do you attend? Have you received Jesus Christ as your Lord and Savior? Have you been baptized in Jesus' name? Do you believe in speaking in tongues? Questions like this would also act as a deterrent especially if I was not interested in the guy. Yes, I am guilty – I used Jesus as a roadblock.

I had recently broken off a relationship with someone at the beginning of the summer. I decided to focus all my energy on my studies, and of course, developing and maintaining a closer relationship with the Lord. I was not looking to get into another relationship. At that point, I was not looking to date any guy at all, let alone an unsaved one. I went about my days, studying and working. My goal was to get into the nursing program. Everyone knew I studied. I would literally work in the back office, taking breaks to study for the class, particularly, organic chemistry.

I worked with a great group of people. At times, we had major mailing projects where a group of us gals and guys would sit around as we worked in an assembly-line collating documents, stuffing, and sealing envelopes to mail off to prospective students. Around that table was where we had some of our most interesting conversations. It was really an easy way to get to know people in a friendly and laid-back setting.

Before you continue reading, I would like to mention a disclaimer. Back then, I did not know if a guy was interested in me if he did not explicitly say so. I was a friendly person and did not consider myself to be flirtatious. If a guy was friendly towards me, I took it as if he was just being friendly. So, when my friend pulled me aside and mentioned that she thought Ralph (not his real name), liked me, I thought, *no he doesn't. Besides, he only dates white girls.* Yes, I thought that.

With this new information, I found myself thinking, *hmm, what if he does like me?* I must admit he was cute and my type. He had curly hair, but clean cut. He dressed rather preppy, and he was smart. I did not like dumb guys.

After that, I found myself making sure I looked extra nice when going into work. Putting on lip gloss, making sure my hair was in a cute style, and always having gum handy so my breath would be minty fresh just in case he sat next to me at the worktable. Clearly, I was attracted to him and yes, my friend was right, he was attracted to me.

I knew Ralph wasn't a regular churchgoer. We had been co-workers and friends for a few quarters by this time. As weeks progressed in the fall quarter, he started asking me to go out on dates with him, and I would politely decline. I wanted to go out with him, but I just couldn't get over the fact that we were unevenly yoked. I didn't bombard him with the streamline of questions that I would ask other guys in order to get them to leave me alone because I didn't want him to run away. I wanted Ralph to like me. I liked the attention he was giving me, and I didn't want it to stop.

He was persistent in his asking and so one day he came to me as I sat at the front desk and said, "Let me take you out on a date. You get to pick where we go. Come on just one date." This time I didn't say no, but what I said was, "I tell you what, if I pass my organic chemistry midterm with an A, I'll go out with you." I believe I told him we could go skating or bowling.

"Okay," he said as he went away with a smile on his face.

During the days leading up to my midterm, he would ask how my studying was coming along and if I needed a study partner so that I could get that A on the test. I guess that was his attempt of reminding me that we had a date planned. I would let him know it was coming along well and so, he remained hopeful.

There was a part of me that felt like I let down my guard. Here before, I had only dated church guys. I figured if we found ourselves in compromising situations, one of us would hear from the Lord and not allow it to go further than it should. Now, I had agreed to go on a date with a guy that I could potentially fall head over heels for. *What if we found ourselves in a compromising situation*? The burden would be left up to me to hear God because Ralph was not going to listen. He didn't even go to church on a regular basis. How would he hear God?

There you have it, my idea of having someone who was evenly yoked as a safeguard, I put in place just in case I was not able to control my physical desires. If I didn't listen to God, then he would. In hindsight, I see how selfishly I was thinking. That's a lot of responsibility for any guy to have to handle. The temptation is too great.

I believe God speaks to His children in ways that they can comprehend. He speaks in dreams and visions. He speaks by way of promptings. He speaks to us in a small, still voice. He speaks to us by way of His Word. He speaks to us through men and women who are His spokespersons here on the earth. There are times when I have been resistant to His promptings. It is almost as if it's a nagging sensation within the pit of my stomach that is trying to get me to go in a different direction. I felt that sensation not immediately after I agreed to go on the date with Ralph, but a little afterward.

I had time to think about my future date with him. I felt like I should not go on that date. However, I didn't want to hurt him by canceling. It just didn't seem fair to do so. I felt stuck. During this time, I was invited to a church service. There was a guest speaker who was running a revival. I don't remember her name, but she was a firecracker. I liked how she kept it real and raw while delivering her message. She was not intimidated in the least. She was a perfect mixture of hood and anointing.

After delivering the message she proceeded to prophesy over people in the audience. Prophesying is meant for the edification, exhortation, and comfort of the hearer. True prophets speak the heart and mind of God to the person being spoken to. That night in the small store-front church that housed maybe about fifty people comfortably, a woman of God spoke a word of knowledge over my life that gave me peace about a decision that had to be made.

I was sitting in the chair next to my dear sweet auntie who invited me to the service. I wore a canary-yellow and black dress, sheer pantyhose, and high heeled black pumps with my hair in a dangling, full Shirly-temple curls. The speaker called me out. She didn't ask permission to give me a word. She just started speaking. I don't recall everything she said verbatim, but what I do remember is exactly what I needed to hear.

"You have held up a standard," she said, "you are about to make a decision to compromise. Don't compromise." That was all I needed to hear. I had not followed the gut feeling I had and so I believe God was getting His word to me through someone else. The speaker had no idea about my current situation. She didn't know me. That was the first time I had ever seen or heard her.

I received the confirmation I needed. Now I just needed to muster up the confidence to tell Ralph I could not go on the date with him. Honestly, I no longer had the desire to go. I just needed a way out. I got it. Do you remember that organic chemistry midterm I wrote about earlier? Well, even though I studied diligently, I received a B. That was my way out.

After receiving my grade, Ralph came to me as I sat at the front desk in the office. "So how did you do on the test?" he said.

"I got a B. I can't go out on the date," I said.

He couldn't believe that I would not go out with him over one grade, but in the end, he understood, and I didn't compromise.

MS. YVETTE WILLIAMS:
FOR EVERY MOUNTAIN

This song was written for me when I was going through my divorce but carried me through surgeries, strokes, the death of my father 2009, my mother 2017, and most recently my third oldest sister in 2019. Many times, I would sing this song and it was a time of healing and breakthrough for me and other times I knew it was to bless the people.

It's one of those things and situations that has helped me find my true purpose in life. I was born and raised in a small-town East of Seattle, called Yakima, Washington with two brothers, and five sisters. Then in 1989, I fell in love, married, and moved to Southern California within six months. I was so sure he was the one for me but as time went on things changed but one thing remained the same, my love for and faith in God. After ten years and one baby girl later, we ended up moving back to Yakima, for what I thought would be a few months which turned into an incredible ten years! *Whew! Who would have thought?*

During my stay in Yakima, God had specific plans for my life. Yes, I was still singing all over the country, but during that time, God birthed a ministry that I couldn't even imagine in my wildest dreams. It was clear that I was to work with the women. It all started in my home, "the women of purpose and promise!" Every Wednesday night we would meet at my home at 7 pm for prayer and Bible study. When I tell you God met us there every time! It grew and expanded to Mexico and other groups would meet until God let me know this is just the beginning! Each woman would bring their journal, and our focus scripture was **Habakkuk 2:2-4! Write the vision!** It took off and as each woman that spent time in the word, fasting (Daniel's fast) and in His word saw tremendous growth and within a short time, their purpose was clear. For almost five years, God was with us through each women's conference, which stretched us to go back to our own churches and work. To this day, the women are grounded in the word, blessing our own communities, and striving for more in GOD! We realized that we are destined for greatness as God continues to lead us. God was very clear when He said, "I have a vested interest in you!" *Whew, my God, it still gives me chills.* I know without a shadow of a doubt that God has more in store, and I do not want to take any dream, ministry, vision, or promise to my grave. I want to leave empty and lives completely changed. This woman that God allowed you minister to the masses also knows that I am definitely "A woman of purpose and promise!" I say no, you get your dream back, finish that book, you are equipped to do what God has placed in you.

Habakkuk 2:2, 3, 4: Write the vision, make it plain on tablets so that the runner may read it. There is still a vision for the appointed time. It seems to tarry, wait for it, it will surely come. Hallelujah.

You are a woman of purpose. Blessings.

DR. YVETTE A. JACKSON: CAREGIVER CHRONICLES

C aregiving has been one of the most challenging as well as rewarding snippets in my life thus far. It allowed me to understand the magnitude and all aspects of being a caregiver as well as the perks of understanding and embracing the caregiver experience. **Isaiah 41: 13(NIV) says, "For I the Lord thy God will hold thy right hand, saying unto thee, Fear not; I will help thee. This scripture reflects my journey as a caregiver.**

As a child, my mother was the matriarch of the family. Growing up in a single-parent household, she was the epitome of strength, patience, providing, etc. She made sure that all our needs were met as children, and I never recall any struggle. If she did encounter some challenges, it was never portrayed in her demeanor. She was always a sweet, kind, gentle, soft-spoken mother and this I carry within my heart daily.

Let me just take you back thru my "caregiver chronicles." It began approximately 25 years prior when my mother began to experience some signs of dementia. At that time, she was living in her primary residence with my sister and her family. I recall going to visit her one day, and as she was in the process of dressing herself, I could see by looking at her back that she had lost a considerable amount of weight. I'm not sure if she was refusing to eat or if she was forgetting to eat. Nevertheless, I realized at that point something was wrong.

As time passed, my sister moved and I moved back into my mother's residence along with my three sons (Mitchell age nine, Andrew age seven, and Antoine Jr. age two) to be her primary caregiver. As a single parent, it was as if I had added a fourth child. Although mom at that time was still able to handle her ADLs (Activities of Daily Living) and IADLs (Independent of her Activities of Daily Living), i.e., dressing, bathing, feeding, cleaning, and clothing herself, the disease began to progress a little each day.

She started to forget things like where she put her purse, her money, how to warm her food in the oven, etc. I recall going into her room one day and she was trying to dress herself. She had her slip on her head, and her underwear at her feet, and when I walked into her room, I said, "Hi mom, what are you doing?"

Her response was, "I'm trying to get dressed but I think I'm losing my mind." At that point, I began to help her and assured her that she was okay and that she was not losing her mind. I realized that it was important that I did not make her feel as if she was incompetent, thus I reassured her that everything was okay.

I believe this was a defining moment when I realized that I needed someone to help me with her care, a caregiver. **Philippians 4:13 reads, "I can do all things through Christ which strengthen me."** This scripture reflects my testament during this time as it was a transition of my mindset taking place, spiritually, emotionally, and psychologically. I had to shift my thought process to understand that I could no longer look at our relationship as me being her daughter and she being the mother. Although this was the biological makeup of my being, it was no longer something that I could adhere to. In other words, the roles had to be switched. Of course, my respect for her as my mother was always there, but I had to be the mother and her, the daughter in retrospect. Therefore, I had to be her eyes, ears, etc. to ensure that her wellbeing was maintained.

I began to make some adjustments as to what would happen with her each day as my children went to school and I went to work. I began to look for adult day care programs as I didn't want her to sit in the house every day, and I thought it best that she be around her peers. I went to several locations to find a day program for her and found the best place. Because she was used to going to the senior center daily, I took her with me to find a place. We went to an adult day care, and it was nice. I liked it. Little did I know that mom did not. She told me "I'm not going there. Those people are crazy." So, I waited a few months and took her back and praise God she had no problem with it. There was a small number of people, and the place was immaculate. Therefore, I secured arrangements for her to attend adult day care.

As I was unable to get my three sons off to school, mom to the adult day care (ADC), and myself off to work in a timely manner, I hired someone to come in each morning, bath, dress, and transport her to the ADC, and I would pick her up after work. Fortunately, mom had a sweet demeanor about her thus making it easy to have a caregiver come in and assist her with no resistance.

I recall just one day that she gave the ADC director a hard time. I believe they tried to get her to put her purse down and she hit him with her cane. I got a call that I needed to come as she was violent. Funny thing, this happened only one day and never again. At that point, I sent the purse with her with nothing in it so it would not be an issue as long as she could physically have a purse of her own.

It was a blessing to be the primary caregiver for my mother and her sweet demeanor made it that much more of a pleasurable experience. I know that others who have had this experience may not have had the most enjoyable experience as some who are afflicted with this ailment, dementia/Alzheimer's Disease can be aggressive, combative, etc., and therefore, I am grateful that my mother's journey was as such. The routine became standard, the caregiver would oversee her in the morning, Monday thru Friday, and I would oversee her in the evening and weekends.

Then things began to progress. Mom started experiencing "sundowners' syndrome" which is basically where your loved one mixes up their days and nights. Thank God I had an alarm on the house. I recall early one morning at approximately 3 am, the alarm went off attached to the front door. It was so loud that it woke everyone in the house. I jumped out of bed and mom was fully dressed and had opened the front door. Had it not been for the alarm, she would have been gone and I would not have had a clue as to where she was. She told me that she saw someone outside, by my car. When I looked out of the window, there was no one there. By the grace of God, I was able to get her to relax on the couch with her newspaper (which she read daily) and allow me to go back to sleep. Of course, I reset the alarm so if she opened the door again, I would know.

As time passed, mom began to get more confused. Some of my friends and neighbors would help out with her care. If I had to go shopping, they would come and sit with her. Upon my return from shopping, the neighbor/friend informed me that my mother kept asking for me. She became agitated when I was not there. It became increasingly difficult for me to leave her.

During the summer when my children were on break from school, I would often take them to Palm Canyon Resort in Palm Springs, California to stay for one or two weeks. This particular time I took Mom, my three sons, and I believe my niece went with us also. We had a condo that was fairly small. We usually had a three-bedroom Condo when we went but because of the late reservation, we had a smaller unit. I'm not sure if you are aware of this but when you take your loved one out of their familiar environment and their dementia/Alzheimer's Disease is in the middle stages, they become very confused. Staying at the resort for several days had a profound effect on mom. After a few days, she told me, "I'm going to call my daughter Yvette to come and get me." I responded to her and said, "okay." Although she was talking about me *to me*, she did not recognize that it was me. This was a time where she was unable to be left alone, so I would take her everywhere and I do mean, everywhere with me.

As the disease progressed, there were other extenuating circumstances which forced me to make a decision to move out of her home. As my sons were vastly becoming teenagers, I had to get them in a neighborhood that was more conducive to the needs of teens. Thus, I made the difficult decision to move mom and my sons to another area.

This move resulted in a significant decline in mom's overall ability to perform ADLs and IADLs. She stopped walking and eating soon after the move. I contacted her doctor and told him of her rapid decline. He immediately began Home Health and sent a Nurse and Physical Therapist (PT) to the residence to see her and provide services. The PT was able to get her walking again for a while.

As I was concerned about her getting up in the middle of the night to use the lavatory, I slept in the bed next to her, as I was sure that if she awakened, I would know and be able to assist her as necessary. One morning, I woke up and she was in the closet trying to get to the bathroom. I then redirected her to the bathroom. At that point, I realized that she needed some additional help. I called her doctor and informed him that I was unable to sleep as mom was getting up throughout the night, increasingly confused and that she was keeping me up at night. The doctor then placed the order for a hospital bed, wheelchair, walk, shower chair, trapeze bar, commode to be sent to the residence. The next day, all of the equipment was delivered to our residence. What a relief this was as Mom could sleep in the hospital bed and the rails would be there for her to hold onto and keep her from falling out of the bed.

Having the responsibility of three sons, two of which were teenagers at the time, working a full-time job, going to school full-time, and having to hire, monitor, and excuse caregivers for mom was a unique experience. I was blessed to have two ladies from Belize join as live-in caregivers. They took care of mom as if she was their mother. They even told me to go and take care of my sons and all of the other responsibilities I had and not to worry about mom as they were going to make sure all of her needs were met and thus they did so. They did everything for Mom, and I did not have to worry about anything. They would even cook, clean, etc. What a blessing they were during this time in my life. I'm a firm believer that God will send the right people at the right time in our lives in His divine timing. **Psalm 46:1 read, "God is our refuge and strength, a very present help in trouble."** As I continued to ensure the wellbeing and safety of my mother and my sons, God carried me thru as He always made sure that caregivers were pleasant and did their best to help as much as they could. Of course, there were a few caregivers who were not a good fit, but all things considered, the majority of them were perfect and I thank God for this as it was truly a blessing to be able to continue my routine and not have to worry about the care my mother was receiving.

As a caregiver of my mother for nine years, I was privy to all aspects of caregiving, from the onset of her illness until she succumbed. She was cared for in the home and by the grace of God, I never had to place her in a facility. I know that God our Father will provide all our needs if we just trust and believe in Him. He is our strength when we are weak and per **2 Corinthians 12:9 NIV, "And he said unto me, my grace is sufficient for thee; for my strength is made perfect in weakness. Most gladly therefore will I rather glory in my infirmities, that the Power of Christ may rest upon me."**

This blessed experience was a gift that mom left me. This gift has allowed me to help others or their loved ones who are in the midst of a healthcare challenge or crisis. I have often been called upon by many to give guidance, direction, and reference to all aspects of caregiving. I have taken this knowledge one step further by developing an online course reflective of this gift. The gift, "caregiver chronicles" is an eight-week online course providing a step-by-step walkthrough of caregiving, caretaking, providing, and overseeing process of another. This course is also for the loved one who has some health challenges and may be searching for some guidance and direction as to what to do. It also entails a weekly live platform – Friday Night Live "Ask Dr. Yvette anything" to allow others to share their experience, ask questions, and be a source of support for anyone. Caregiver chronicles is not just for the caregiver, it is for anyone, family, friend, etc. It is a place.

If you or someone you know is in need of help, guidance, direction, or just want to share their experience, please share my contact information with them and I will be happy to assist them.

Godspeed to you and yours. If you will allow us to, we will be happy to help you develop your "caregiver chronicles." Blessings!

Licensed Clinical Social Worker
Honorary Doctorate in Ministry

DENEEN MILNER:
IT'S ME...MY STORY

Today, I am a Licensed Vocational Nurse and have been working in healthcare since 1988. I started in health care. Believe it or not, because of watching TV, I saw a commercial that said everything I needed to hear. I work for one of the leading healthcare organizations as a senior project manager, LVN in the Clinical Education Department. I cannot believe, I work with a team of five registered nurses and one senior medical assistant, and when my position was created and posted, I was the one to get the job in the end. The wonderful feeling of accomplishment came over me. I have come so far to arrive in this career of teaching all clinical staff, all current and future healthcare policies, procedures, and new protocols (COVID safety training). *How did I get here*? Let me take you back a bit to my childhood and as a teenage mother.

I was born at John Wesley Hospital Los Angeles, California August of 1964. I am sure it was a hot day because every birthday I have had, it has been a hot day. I was the second born, the first girl. My mother had three more children, one brother before me and one sister, and a brother after me. I had lots of company during my childhood, from my siblings and my parent's siblings had children as well. Our family get-togethers were awesome, in that, we were able to see all our cousins. Those were the best days. I remember dancing for a quarter against my cousins for my granny. We would have the best food cooked from scratch from my granny and my aunt. Looking back, my heart smiles for all the memories, remembering my granny who loved me better than I could put in words. I was my granny's favorite, and she was mine. My granny's house is where we all met up, especially on Sundays after church. Granny cooked every Sunday. I couldn't wait for Sundays, to see all the family.

My mom married a wonderful man, who took on her and her three children. My mom and dad later had a son together, which made four of us. My dad and mom raised us as best as they could. My mom being incredibly old fashioned in her ways, we all had to sit up properly, keep your hair neat, and keep your dress down and our legs closed. The latter was my mother's talk about sex. I was raised in the church starting at the age of eight years old. We went to church a lot (three to four times a week and all weekend long). My dad became a pastor and then a bishop. Everyone in our household had a job in the church, whether it was in the choir, the usher board, the church revival week, the church drill team, Sunday school, serving communion, etc. We were strong churchgoers up until I was about 16 or 17 years old. We were at the church so much we knew everyone there. It was mandatory to stay after church, while mom and dad greeted all the deacons, and first ladies of the church. They greeted and spoke to the pastor of the church to the leader of the minister boards and the bible teachers. We were well established in the church.

Here, at this church, at the age of 15 years old, I found myself really becoming mitten with a guy. I thought he was so cute, and he dressed and smelled nice, also had his own car. I was so impressed. We talked and I thought, *Wow I cannot believe this guy is talking to me and he likes me*. One day, I decided I will let him go all the way because I did not want him to go elsewhere. I slept with him one time and I thought then, that was horrible. *Was sex supposed to hurt? Why am I bleeding? Oh my God, I cannot ask anyone what to do.* I was scared and I knew I was never going to have sex again even if he goes elsewhere. I was ready to break up with him if he ever asked me to have sex again. Sex was not for me. I did not care for that type of trauma. I wanted to have something to talk about with my friends but ended up keeping it a secret. I did not want anyone to know about my horrible experience and was hoping they could tell by looking at me, that I had sex. *I would just die, please God give me my virginity back. I promise to NEVER have sex again.* The things you think as a child.

Three months, after the sexual encounter, my mother asked me if I am putting on weight. I said not that I know of. I was not aware of my body changes at this age. Then my mother asked why was I eating everything in the house? I said, "I don't know mom, I guess I am hungry from running track." Track was one of the high school sports, I participated in. Then my mom asks if I had sex? My heart fluttered. I could not breathe. I was looking wide-eyed, I had a lump in my throat, and I am scared to answer. I turn to my mother, and look as if I was surprised, she is asking me if I had sex. I of course said, no. I could not tell her the truth, I was so afraid. My mom then stated to me, "If I find out you had sex, I am going to kill you with my bare hands." I swallowed hard and said, "yes ma'am." Now I am worried, not knowing my body or how to tell I was pregnant.

Weeks later, we have choir practice, and we are getting ready to go to the church. I pull out my favorite blue skirt to wear. I put on my top and then the skirt and I reach back to zip my skirt up, but the zipper will not go up. I struggle and struggle to pull my zipper up. No luck, so I asked my sister to help me. She pulls and pulls but no success. My sister says to me, "You're getting thicker sis, now you won't be so skinny." I cried because I did not understand why I could not get in my favorite blue skirt which I wore often.

At the doctor's appointment, my mom felt my sister and I are at the age to have our first female health exam such as pap smears and maybe try birth control to regulate our cycles. I was happy about birth control because I already had a situation where I could've used them. It is my turn to be examined and the doctor is coming to the completion of the exam. The doctor does one last pelvic palpation and I can feel a hard knot in my stomach. It really scared me because I had never felt anything like that in my stomach before. The doctor tells my sister and I to get dress and he will be back with our test result and the birth control we will start on. The doctor returns and calls out my sister's name and says she is positive pregnant and that I was negative and could start the birth control. I was almost going to exhale, and my sister jumps up and say, "No, I cannot be pregnant, I have not had sex before."

The doctor re-examines his medical records, then states, "I am sorry, Deneen is positive pregnant, and my sister was negative." I was instantly devastated by what was happening. I was thinking about how my mother was going to kill me, what will my dad say? What will my granny say? And what will the members of the church say? I was thinking, *when we get outside, I will run in the streets and get hit by a car and I will lose the baby. I cannot have a baby now. I have no clue of how to care for a baby. Oh God, help me! My mom is going to kill me, and I will not get to see the baby anyway.*

I slowly look over at my mom after the doctor leaves the room. She is smiling at me. I was confused. I look down and then back up at my mother's face to what she could be thinking and when will she let me have it. She is still smiling, and she says "So, you gonna make me a granny? I am so happy. Now, who is the father?" I was very truthful with my mother, telling her what I had done and with who. She was understanding and excited about the future of being a granny.

The call to the father of my baby was not easy. I spoke to him a little just making conversation because I was scared to tell him that I was expecting his child. I drew up courage from somewhere and just told him. He was silent, then started to stutter asked me if I was sure. I told him I went to the doctor and what occurred at the doctor's office. He was again silent and then said, "How do you know I am the father?" My heart began to race, I answered, "because you were the only person, I have ever had sex with." He said, "Did you have another boyfriend before me maybe it is his baby." I was in tears. I couldn't believe he was not going to take responsibility. What am I going to do now? I told my mom and the good thing about a mother that knows everyone in the church, she knew my baby's father's mother too. My mother had a conversation with my baby's father's mother, and I do not think it went well. My mother told me not to worry about my child's father being a part of her life. He did not want to own up to his responsibility. The best thing I had ever heard. Yet, I was still terribly upset that my child would not know her father.

I was 28 weeks pregnant, and I had contractions all night. I asked my mom to take me to the hospital because the pain was getting worse. I arrived at my delivering hospital and the doctor checks me. He tells my mother and I, "the baby is coming, and this hospital is not equipped to take on a baby at 28-week gestation." The hospital asked my mother to take me to another hospital which is better equipped, Cedar Senai Hospital. The nurses were awesome, and they stopped the pain. The nurses consistently checked my progress and tried to slow my contractions, thus keeping the baby from coming out too soon. I watched all those nurses take care of me and that is where I began to dream of being a nurse. I wanted to open the equipment and apply it to my patients and make them feel just as good as they were making me feel.

My little girl was born only 2lbs and 2oz. She had all ten fingers and toes. She had the tiniest toenails and fingernails. She could not fit a newborn diaper. Her suckling reflections were not strong, and she would get tired of suckling, so tube feeding was introduced to help her. My daughter was not able to go home with me, and I was devastated. She was under-weight and needed time to stay in the hospital to get bigger and stronger. This child was a fighter, she almost lost her life twice. She got jaundice but I touched my little baby and I asked God to change it. I told God how sorry I was for not wanting her in the beginning. I apologized for how I created her, out of wedlock. I told God if He would help this precious angel that He sent here for me to take care of, I would always make sure I do. Two days later, my baby got better and started lifting her head. I was at the hospital daily, talking to her and singing to her, "you are my sunshine my only sunshine." I wanted my baby to know my voice. She would look for me when she heard me, and I was so proud of that. 4lbs 10oz two months after birth, and my little princess got to come home. Thank you, Jesus!

My daughter is now two years old. She was born with a hole in her heart and now it must be repaired. I am scared because the odds of my child surviving the surgery at that time was 50%. I thought these odds were 50% in my favor because I know God – if I do not know anything else. I prayed, I called the church warriors, and my baby survived. My daughter grew up without any deformities. She has one scar on her scalp area where her largest vein was for the intravenous therapy, she needed during her first two months stay at the hospital. My daughter today is a healthy, happy 40-year-old woman who holds a bachelor's degree in healthcare management and an associate degree in healthcare office administration.

Life has a way of taking you through journeys and roads we are all uncertain if it is the right way to go. Trust God through it all and never lose your faith. God will do what He says He will do. He took a little girl that believed in Him and brought her through one of the biggest changes in my life. Today, I am proud to say through raising my daughter and making sure she survives, I went back to school and received dual AS degrees one for administration of justice and the other for correctional science. I also hold my nursing license. Do not be afraid to get knowledge, I have found it is power. I was not a straight-A student. I failed in high school and then finally I dropped out due to my pregnancy. When I laid eyes on my daughter everything changed for me, willpower came from nowhere. I asked God for His strength and He brought me through, my G.E.D, college, and through nursing school and now as a healthcare educator. Get up and keep standing.

Senior Project Manager, LVN
Clinical Education Department
Healthcare Organization

QUEEN LENNIE WOODLEY:
I AM A SURVIVOR

Throughout most of my life, there was an onslaught of things that I needed to overcome. There was a period of time I experienced abuse, addiction, and even homelessness.

My addiction, which devastated my life, homelessness, lack of self-esteem, and no hope. I found recovery the best that ever happened in my life...I found hope, *I found me.*

Most of my recovery began on Skid Row which addicts call the "belly of the beast." In 2006, I had to get control of my life. With this change of heart and mind, my life changed for the better. I was still homeless and living on Skid Row, with no job, skills, or aspirations – I had a change of heart and mind and decided to attend Los Angeles City College where I graduated Suma Cum Laude and became a member of the International Honor Society, Phi Theta Kappa and of the National Honor Society of Psychology PSI BETA in 2009.

I quickly began working with the homeless population to provide adequate housing to dislocated families, while providing substance abuse counseling. I found my passion in helping my community and became a licensed addictions specialist for the state of California

In 2011, Shields for Families hired me. I helped re-unifying mothers and their children working with the Department of Social Services to assist families to be drug-free, self-sustaining, and productive members of society, which was a natural high that I never experience before or ever known.

I believe that the damaged and the broken can be healed. I know that to have a voice is a sense of freedom. I also understand that with the right resources and support anything is possible, because...*I am a living testimony of change.*

Instead of abusing drugs, I became an advocate for those with this addiction. I became a substance abuse counselor for the Los Angeles County Department of Mental Health.

I had a low self-esteem, now I am working with people with mental illness to cross barriers of stigma by enhancing self-esteem and self-pride. My sense of community grew more when I became an advocate for the Keith Bursey Jr. family in 2017 because he had no more voice and was shot and killed by an LAPD officer. I fought for accountability, transparency, and justice for my community.

I am a survivor...And I know that you too can survive these same challenges in life.

FAYE EDMOND:
MY STORY THROUGH FAITH, PRAYER AND PERSEVERANCE

I had thought about many stories to share, but one came to mind from when I resided in Chicago, Illinois. It's a story of much prayer and perseverance through the storm. Yes, we have many storms, but it is how you are going to come out at the end of the storm.

In the early '90s, I worked at Chicago State University. I was downsized from IBM. Yes, that is correct, downsized. At any rate, I began looking for employment as I just began receiving my unemployment compensation. I was hired as a temporary worker to work 900 hours. I worked in the administrative department which I loved very much. The office I worked in worked very closely with the president of the University. Dr. Cross. Chicago State University is a predominately black university. I loved working with our African American sisters and brothers. It was a huge change coming from the corporate world and truly a culture shock!

I worked very hard at my duties, and I *ALWAYS* assisted my immediate supervisor. Whatever she needed or called my name from her office, I was there for her. However, she became very abusive with the tone of her voice. I did not know why. When she would talk to me or give me a directive, it was harsh at times. She would stand over me while I was sitting in my chair at my desk. Yes, she was African American. Regardless of her tone, I treated her with respect. As time passed, my supervisor, Sandra would call me from her office with a loud voice asking me to help her with whatever was going on with her computer, or just asking me when I would be completed with my assignments. My co-workers began to take notice of how Sandra would yell at me or call me loudly from her office. I sat right outside of her office so there was no need to yell for me.

Sandra continued this abusive way of talking to me. Word began to spread to other co-workers, and they would tell me, "Why is Sandra yelling at you?" I would say, "I don't know. I guess she must be having issues."

Sandra's abusive language towards me began to take a toll on me. I began to hate to go to work. We worked on the third floor at Chicago State University. I would think about pushing Sandra out of the third-floor window. I wanted to put her out of my misery and her misery too! I would get stomach pains because I did not want to face her or deal with her yelling at me. Like I said above, she would stand over me giving me directions, and her boobs would be in my face. By the way, in my opinion, when people stand over you in a derogatory way, it gives them power over you. I did not like that because she had power over me. Further, she could fire me as well. So, I felt sort of trapped. I went to human resources and reported Sandra due to her harassment and intimidation. Guess what? One of the human resource representatives told me that they could not do anything because I was on probation. I thought that was ludicrous, as I had never heard of such nonsense. Well, I figure if the human resource was not going to do anything, then I was on my own. I am going to fast forward.

Sandra called a meeting that included me, and the director of the department, and of course Sandra. Sandra was telling a lot of lies in the meeting stating that I was not doing my work or some stuff she was making up. I told the director that I do my work all the time and get it done. Well, a couple of days later, Sandra told me that I needed to look for employment elsewhere on campus because it was not working out. This was like in the middle of the week. Yes, Sandra fired me! So, I was home just two days, and I received a call from Sandra. She stated that she needed me to come back to work because she did not hire anyone. Therefore, I was back at work. My co-workers asked me why I came back to work under Sandra knowing what she did to me. I told my co-workers I needed a job because I had to take care of my child and pay the bills.

I began looking for employment on campus. Every time there was an opening for administrative opening, I would go on the interview on campus. I mean I was running from one end of the campus to the next. I felt it in my spirit that my time was going to run out with Sandra, and I did not want to be put in that situation again. I know my GOD is able and can do exceedingly abundantly above all that we can ask or think of!

In my apartment bathroom you can walk into the bathroom closet. You have heard of a prayer closet. Well, my bathroom closet was my prayer room. I needed help from God!! I could not handle Sandra, but I knew God could. I prayed earnestly in my prayer closet. I sat on the floor in the bathroom closet and prayed and cried out to the Lord. I needed God's help to work on me and to work on Sandra. By this time, Sandra had given me an ending date to leave again. Well, I just stood on God's word that He would help me through my adversity and bless me with the income so that I can continue to care for my family. *Guess what*? I went to another interview in the education department. Dr. Fernandez hired me on the spot – it was just like that! The day Sandra told me bye-bye, God had blessed me with the position in the education department. I started the new position the next day. Although the salary was much lower than I had previously received, I was so excited. I was starting all over again. I knew God was in control and He was doing something big. He took me out of the clutches of my supervisor, Sandra. At any rate, I did not lose any time from work. *Hallelujah, hallelujah praise God!* Prayer works and continues to work!

There was a pay cut! But you know what, God had another plan for me. I worked my butt off in the education department. It was a privilege and honor to work in the education department because I worked with professionals, and they did not tolerate "mess." I worked very closely with the department chairperson and the entire staff in the education department. They loved my work and gave me praises.

I ensured all the teachers had their paperwork copied for exams/tests and so forth. I continued to look at the hiring board to see if additional positions/promotions were available. I worked in the education department for a while.

I applied to another position on campus in another department and was hired. I did very well and worked very hard. I continued to look for positions with higher pay because I determined to regain my status as an administrative secretary, the same position that Sandra had me fired from. *Guess what*? Another position was posted, and it was an administrative secretary position. I applied for the position and was hired. It was a new office starting from the ground up. Soon after, the leadership changed, but that was okay. The department I worked in benefitted minorities in the science, technology engineering, and mathematics fields.

One day, I went to lunch and came back to my office. On my desk was a message on a pink message note. The message was for my supervisor. The message was from Sandra. She wanted my supervisor to call her. I provided my supervisor with the note. My supervisor shared with me that she needed to hire someone to do the marketing and communication portion of the position. I shared with my supervisor the circumstances regarding Sandra and me. I also shared and suggested to my supervisor during the interview process, if Sandra is the best candidate for the position, then she should hire Sandra.

Sandra was hired for the position, but she was not my supervisor. News of Sandra's hire in my department reached a lot of people on campus. People were asking me if Sandra was my supervisor and I said, "no!" I shared with my colleagues that I reported to Dr. Comer.

I greeted Sandra with open arms. I did not have any ill feelings against Sandra. I just knew she was no longer my supervisor, and I was very happy about that. Dr. Comer called a staff meeting. It was Robert, Dr. Comer, Sandra, and me. Dr. Comer explained what each person was responsible for then she dropped the bomb! She said that Sandra will be reporting to ME! *Did you all hear that*! I did not know what to say or do. The room became silent. Dr. Comer was not playing either. She told Sandra that she had to report to me if she was not coming into work and some other things. But the fact that she said Sandra must report to me was like *OH MY GOD*! Remember how I shared with you how Sandra had treated me so badly.

God will fix it in HIS own timing. It is all about GOD! This is the same lady who lied on me and fired me and then needed me to come back to work, which I did. God will always win, and He will fight your battles, every time!

Look at God! What He has done for me, God will do it for YOU and others! Sandra did not last long in the office. She did not call in when she was supposed to report for work. I had informed Dr. Comer about what was going on. She told me that she told Sandra it was not working out and gave her the time off to find another job. Sandra had worked in the office with me for about five or six months.

God will make a way out of no way! Quitting was not an option for me. I had to wait on GOD! **Isaiah 40:31 KJV says,** *"But they that wait upon the LORD shall renew their strength; they shall mount up with wings as eagles; they shall run, and not be weary; and they shall walk and not faint."*

This is my testimony of faith, prayer, and perseverance.

PASTOR FRANCHESCA LONG:
I OVERCAME AND BROKE THE MOLD

Growing up I was very sheltered by my mother. I knew my father but did not have a huge relationship with him because he lived so far away. My mother worked multiple jobs to make sure my siblings and I were properly cared for, and my brother had a change of plans. Being the middle child of three was pushed to becoming more mature than what I should have been. My mother was a huge enforcer of chores and was adamant about them being done. I had no other choice but to grow up and get things done.

I was taught things such as doing laundry, cooking, cleaning, and caring for my younger sibling. But I knew in my heart there was so much more to life than that. I wanted to be a lawyer at one point, then a police officer all because I did not see many women like them. Growing a bit older while being raised around the church, (not in, but around) I grew a fascination with the word of God. There were a lot of things that I grew up watching and just knew I did not want them to be a part of my life.

Like some people who do not understand why their life is going a certain way, I became confused, depressed, and suicidal. There was so much more going on than just this bit here, however this is where I made a pivotal change in my life for the better. I was going to Church of Christ, and I began to feel a deeper hunger as well as a drawing to understanding God and the word of God. This hunger I was feeling was so much stronger than the depression and thoughts of suicide and I wanted to discover why. So, I began to study the word of God and sleep with scriptures next to my pillow for comfort. Soon after I heard the Lord calling me in my sleep. Just as in **1 Samuel 3:8, "And the Lord called Samuel again the third time. And he arose and went to Eli, and said, 'here am I, for thou didst call me.' And Eli perceived that the Lord had called the child."**

Because I didn't know at that time what was transpiring in my life and hearing the Lord call me; I went to an Elder in the church and asked why I would hear such a thing. After revealing to the Elder that I felt in my spirit that God was calling me into Ministry I was told God did not call women. During that time, I was close to my Sunday school teacher and went for further information because it just was not settling that God just didn't call women. God showed Himself to me in more than one way during this time dealing with my mental and emotional state regarding how I felt about myself and my family. I believe that the Lord was calling me because no woman in my family was sensitive enough spiritually to be able to hear such a thing be done.

Then I encountered a close friend of mine Having the Holy Spirit run around a church service in the excitement of what was heard, The Word of God. After the service, I inquired what was he doing and why was he running around the church. And he shared he had the Holy (Holy Spirit) Ghost. I became most curious; because the last time I had saw anything as such I was a little girl. And my family now went to a church that did not believe it took all of the running, jumping, and shouting to become free of the mental and emotional bondage that still plague many to this day. What I found most amusing was the freedom of expression by using the body.

After seeing a friend filled with the Holy Ghost, we became closer because I believed I was able to ask some of the questions I had about the Bible and the consistent dreams I had been having. I really didn't know what God was doing with this whole situation or if he even knew who I was. I had so many questions and had no idea how to even start asking. All I know at this point in my life was that I found a church and a people who could possibly answer the many questions that I had, about God and the Bible. I couldn't even imagine that my life was getting ready to change so drastically.

I had a talk with my mother because I was in my youth and I expressed to her that I was desiring more spiritual growth then what was being provided to me. So, after speaking with my friends (my now husband) grandmother she allowed me to start attending church with them. I began to grow spiritually and joined the choir and attend Youth Bible Studies. I then found out what a real relationship with the Lord was. That it was a posture of the heart, and when the Lord is in your heart everything else begins to make sense. Not perfect but it makes sense.

Now, let's really examine this thing; what most people would think is that when you get saved that everything becomes golden. Sorry to have to reinform you but for most who have a call on their life, things are getting ready to be testy for you. When you come into the knowledge of Christ and don't have mentors to walk you through the process, and the ones that are willing you push them away because of former hurts, you set yourself up to make mistakes because of your fleshly desires. The feelings of suicide and depression had left but I was now open to feelings of intimacy and what the Bible calls fornication. My friend and I engaged in premarital sex, causing my attitude as a teen to be haywire. I ended up pregnant multiple times having one abortion, a miscarriage, and a child out of wedlock. And let's just set the record straight, he was the only one that I had been messing with. My heart was open on so many levels and exposed to many spirits in operation because I refused to receive correction and proper love by the mothers who attempted to help.

We're just looking onto the surface on this thing, but the root of it is the issues I had with my mother and my father. I was looking for solutions to love and acceptance in the wrong places. And when certain people attempted to use them as a scapegoat for the relationships that I longed to have with many. Well, that was just the beginning of where we were going.

After having our first child we figured we would need to settle our lives. We moved in with one another and started living together, thinking it would be healthy. Well, we weren't happy and my boyfriend was not only seeing me at the time. I found myself pregnant fighting my emotions and now my soon to be child's father who I believed would one day be my husband. Not only were we verbally fighting but physically also. There was so much that happened during this pregnancy causing me to go into early labor and my son being born almost two months early. I ended up having to leave my son in the hospital for two weeks and I then made up my mind that I wanted more for my life than just a family and emotional security. I needed to start my career. My dream career from the age of 12 was to become a stylist, both with hair and clothing. While my son was in the hospital, I enrolled in cosmetology school and waited until spring classes to start. My life was falling in line, so I thought, there was still a huge part messing. Started school and I began to see what real life was and still with all of this going on. We stayed faithful to church and now that we have a son, we began to be faithful to one another.

We were off to a great start. We had gotten an apartment and moved in with one another I was in school and working a part-time job and he was working full-time. I wanted more, I needed more, and I was going for everything that my hopes and dreams aspired to do. I was ready for the rest of my life to begin. School was going well, and we began to talk about marriage again. I had shared with my boyfriend/child's father multiple times that I didn't just want to live with someone but I wanted to be a wife and have in the works businesses and projects that would be different from what I had seen my entire life. What I found out is that we shared some of the same desires and later that year we had gotten married.

We are married with a child, and I believe progressing. Even at this time, we launched a church. We were only 19 and looking at the rest of our lives. Things are beginning to fill out and an overwhelming comfort began to form in my thoughts. I am building my relationship with the Lord and building my thoughts to a healthy family. Soon after we found out we were pregnant with our second child, and I had just finished cosmetology school and passed state board and began moving towards my second goal.

During all of this time, we faced homelessness and infidelity as well as lots of family issues. However, we did not want our issues to stop us from growing we actually used our mess as fertilizer to feed what we were growing together. Seeing how we wanted to build a strong family foundation because of the much we had endured in our adolescents. Later, we moved from the Bay Area California to Sacramento, California.

In Sacramento, the Lord began to deal with our personal growth and development as individual people. We sought a councilor in order to have any hope for our relationship. I believe most people have personal issues that are not completely dealt with before getting into what should be permanent relationships. We found it to be very instrumental in our development, for God was getting ready to take us in both life and ministry, both spiritually and supernaturally. At this point in my life, I was attempting to find what the void was in my life that I was feeling. Not that I hadn't already known I just never really deeply explored it.

Spiritually, I was diving into a place where I had never discovered before and as deep as I was getting ready to go. I gained an extensive study, meditation, and prayer life spending hours at a time in supplication. When I wasn't working on clients, I was in my Bible on the search for who this new person was in the Lord was so desperately longing to get to know. See the problem that I continued to run into is that I had dreams and aspirations that I was not willing to give up for the sake of fulfilling this place I was being drawn to spiritually. Not understanding that this place that I was being drawn to was going to enhance where I was going in my personal life. I hadn't paid attention to how I ministered to the emotional and spiritual needs of my clients while they were in my chair and how I was already in pursuit of who the Lord was calling me to be. Those areas I was looking for fulfillment were being met as I continued to dive deeper into meditation and prayer, I was becoming more aware of the completeness of now having a sense of direction towards where I was going.

I started small women empowerment groups encouraging women of all age brackets to pursue their dreams while pursuing a strong relationship with God. I had a longing in my belly to help women learn to be comfortable in their skin and not look for validation from outside sources but learn to be whole from within. To help them to see that if any relationship they wanted to have with other people they would have to learn to be comfortable within themselves. One saying that I live by today is, "If you learn to Love you, other people won't have an issue trying to find ways to like you, it is all about your confidence." What I came to understand is that the only validation I needed was the comfort of who I wanted to be and not of what everyone else expectations were for me. I had to come to grips with the fact that I can only live for me.

This was a valuable lesson for me, seeing how I did not want my children to ever think that they would have to meet the expectations of others. I want them to discover who they are and learn their likes and dislikes and be okay with expressing themselves without violating the peace of others.

After leaving the Bay Area and moving to Sacramento we sat under our spiritual mother for a little over a year, and after the spirit of the Lord spoke and she agreed we launched back into ministry with a new mindset and outlook on addressing others. One thing I learned sitting under her for that time is that sometimes the hurt of growing up will cloud who you really desire to be and who God is calling you to be. I began to shine in a whole new light. Ministry really began to take off and the Lord allowed me to name my personal ministry Truth be Told with Fran, this was the beginning of a blossoming flower and she is still maturating into a full place. Now, sprouting in areas that were once too dark for anything healthy to grow out of a person. Now for some, they tell you to have to retreat in order to remain healthy, but when you have been in darkness most of your life you want to make sure you stay out of that dark place. Find an accountability partner, to make sure all things are done that the father is requesting of us to do.

Sacramento became the place of enhancement for my family. Both my children, my husband, and I began to view life differently and no longer made excuses for the choices that we made.

I received a call that my mother needed assistance because her health was beginning to decline. My husband and I made a conscious decision to move my mother from the Bay to our home in Sacramento. With my mother being there it forced me to deal with the childhood hurts I had even more so, but also assisted in the healing process for my mother.

In the middle of May in 2018, my family encountered death in the family and a few days later my mother suffered a stroke. I, along with my siblings and my grandmother, cared for my mother. While going through the processes with my mother, my family, and I encountering homelessness for a second time, and this time living in our church. We lived in our church for a total of six months and while living there we never gave up hope and didn't stop doing ministry. We decided that we would continue to pursue after God and His plan for our life in the month of November of 2018 the Lord spoke to my husband and told him we needed to leave what we were familiar with and move to Tulsa, Oklahoma. It was extremely hard, I was working full time in a salon, my mother was in a nursing home, and I needed to make sure that my children's livelihood was secure.

Somehow, I knew deep down in my gut that my life was getting ready to become increasingly better. When first getting to Tulsa we lived at a hotel, however, 15 days in, our homelessness was over. I also transferred my cosmetologist license and found a salon to work in, lastly after being here a few months we reopened the ministry. We had received prophetic word while in our transition that when the Lord released us, we would hit the ground running and we did just that.

One thing we have really sought after is remaining focused on what the Lord was calling us to do. And that has helped us through.

I never gave up on my dreams and I chased after God and my identity gaining an understanding that you cannot give up on what you want because life happens.

I came to the understanding that with God, everything was possible. He showed us how to forgive ourselves for the things we couldn't control and to Love ourselves in the areas that seemed most difficult. Even after our bodies changed, God allowed us to see the value of who we were as individuals and to accept the changes that were being made. I learned that no one would ever be able to Love me greater than the Love I had for myself, and that included my husband.

Because I never gave up and my support system, I have opened up a clothing boutique and, in the process, to get things finalized to open my hair salon. My life is still moving in the upward direction and it is all because I chose to continue to pursue the afterlife and fight to get out of the darkness and generational darkness to become greater than what I had seen.

Stay tuned for a more miraculous as you pursue to become a more miraculous you. This is only the beginning.

This is only the beginning...

DEJOIRÉ BENSON:
MY STORY…MY LIFE

My name is DeJoiré Benson. I have been married for 26 years and I have two beautiful daughters, Ericka (34-years-old) and Déja (22-years-old). I was born in Los Angeles, CA. At the age of one, my mother and I moved to St. Louis, where she was from. I grew up in the projects. I did not realize it until years later because I never needed a thing. Though I am the only child of my parents, I have one sister and two brothers, on my father's side. Growing up, he raised them, but he was absent from my life. The pain of his rejection is still painful, to this day. Thank God that I have a Heavenly Father. Also, when I was 21 years old, my mother married my father, Jerry and I gained two younger sisters.

I was raised solely by my mother, Doris Williams, and she instilled some incredible values in me. She stressed the need for me to obtain my degree and she worked hard to put me through college, without any assistance from any other sources. I will be forever grateful to her that I graduated without any student loans.

In 1988, I accepted Jesus Christ as my personal savior at Plain Truth Missionary Baptist Church in Long Beach, CA. Currently, I am a member of Loveland Church in Fontana, CA.

I graduated from Pomona High School then, I earned a Bachelor of Science degree in Business, with an emphasis in Management and Human Resources, from California State Polytechnic University in Pomona, CA. After working in corporate America for a decade, I resigned in 1998 in order to become the primary caregiver for my youngest daughter, Déja, who has special needs. It was devastating for me to have to give up my career. Also, the disappointment of not having a normal mother-daughter relationship with my daughter has been emotionally draining. Thanks to my husband who purchased a Marketing Business and a Travel

159

Business for me over 14 years ago, we have been able to pay off an enormous amount of debt and I was able to raise all three of my credit scores to 850.

In addition, I am also a proud, lifetime member of Delta Sigma Theta, Sorority, Inc., a public service sorority. In addition, I am an advisory board member with Chemo Buddy's, an organization that provides support to patients undergoing chemotherapy treatments.

I believe that it is necessary to saturate oneself with the word of God and to associate with other believers in order to rise above the storms in life that are sure to come! You must truly believe that God works all things for the good of those who love Him and who have been called according to His purpose.

APOSTLE DR. ROSEANNA ROMAN: ADVANCING IN ADVERSE SEASONS

On Aug. 15, 1986, our lives came to a screeching halt, the happiest day in a young couple's life turned into a horrific nightmare! Our son Paul Daniel was born with an incurable brain injury that devastated us beyond our imagination. That morning we entered into the maternity ward, carrying a full-term baby who was already in distress. The doctor told me to come in to be induced and after laboring 15 hours with a high fever and still no baby, a c-section was ordered, and my last recollection was of the anesthesiologist right before I went under. Upon awaking I was taken to the neonatal unit. My first glance of my baby was in an incubator with wires all over his healthy-looking body.

Our lives were forever changed as we met the doctor in his office, our hearts were debilitated and utterly demolished by the doctor's cruel words, "Your son suffered an irreversible brain injury called Cerebral Palsy, he lacked a significant amount of oxygen during the labor process and he will most likely never thrive."

These words hit us like a sledgehammer, they tore and ripped our hearts out of our bodies! After the office visit, I was bowled over in unbearable anguish, grief and sorrow. It was at this moment when I heard a voice from within say, *are you going to believe the doctors or are you going to believe me, whose report will you believe?* When I heard these life-giving words, my reply was, "That's right, I can get a miracle!" Strength and determination entered into my heart and set my life on an immediate course to seek and find the healer, Jesus Christ!

We had to come home without our baby, because he couldn't suckle, nearly a month later he began sucking his bottle and we were able to bring Paul home. We went from doctor visits to doctor visits as the prognosis was confirmed, Paul's vision was seriously impaired, he had no muscle tone, he was unable to hold his head up, his body was floppy and lifeless looking, he had seizures, tumors, great hearing loss and as time went by, he remained in an infant state, with minimal development. His body grew but there was little to no cognitive awareness. He couldn't chew, walk or talk, sit, or stand! The word quadriplegia, which means paralyzed in all four limbs, became a frequently spoken word at our doctor visits. Despite all of this, I felt blessed because Paul was not ill with sickness and he wasn't on any medications or machines.

Cottonwood Christian Center was close by, so I began attending and rededicated my life, (at 17 years old I accepted Christ on a TBN call, but because there was no instance difference, I walked away!) I was water baptized, dedicated Paul to the Lord, and I began weekly bible study, started fasting, baptized in the Holy Spirit, speaking in Tongues, attending Christian Conference's and joined prayer groups! I was eager to begin my new life in Christ and threw myself into a Christian Lifestyle, leaving my old life behind without a reservation! I couldn't get enough of the Word of God!

Heavy grief, sorrow, and fear were still attacking the mind and heart continuously, but hope was starting to bring light back into my dark world. I became a prisoner of HOPE throughout the next 31 years, my hunger for the Word of God was insatiable! The Holy Spirit said to me, "I will heal you first Roseanna and then will heal Paul." I couldn't understand that because I wasn't the one who needed to be healed, Paul was!

Ladies With Purpose

I was an Atheist right before I gave my life to the Lord over 34 years ago. I had severed and seared my God Monitor & Compass, a guide, to keep me on the straight and narrow road, but I chose to ignore and reject the overtures of my God-Given Gift, my conscience. Our conscience forbids lawlessness, reckless behavior, a conscience is a warning and alert system given to every man to keep us moving in the right direction and to keep from moving toward the wide and broad road that leads to destruction.

I became an Atheist after I agreed to have two abortions. I deaden, muzzled, and seared my God-given conscience with a hot branding iron to protect my lifestyle of selfishness, self-will and self-indulgence. You must deaden conscience when you are involved in such horrific acts! In order to cope after I had a third abortion, I proclaimed "There is no God" so that I might not be accountable for my actions and I would stop feeling regret, shame, guilt, embarrassment, or self-loathing.

I was riddled with attacks of anxiety for years, I was certain I was losing my mind or going to die from a heart attack. The pains in my chest were frequent, my breathing labored, as dread, worry and stress were familiar companions. I was nervous, fearful, emotionally unsound and isolated myself socially because I constantly was running to the ladies' room, I couldn't keep any food in my tummy.

Danny and I married because we were with a child before marriage, and I was not going to abort this child so we married. I told Danny of the abortions but neither one of us knew how this would play out in our lives. As we dated, we drank, smoked and cocaine was our drug of choice, until I was pregnant with Paul. After Paul's birth, Danny continued to live heartbroken and unrestrained, as I dedicated myself to God.

My desire for the Word of God was unquenchable, I attended church every Wednesday and Sunday, I loved attending the church where my hope and faith were ever increasing, I loved reading, studying, saturating myself in the Word all day long 24\7. I had the

Word of God playing on my TV, on the radio, on cassette tapes, on my Walkman, it was playing in my house constantly throughout the days, weeks, months and years of Paul's life.

Danny and I had another son three years later, my beautiful son, Tony was born a healthy baby, and I had no reservations that my baby would be born unhealthy because the Word was dwelling in me mightily. Six years later the Holy Spirit said, "I would conceive and have a third child." So at 40 years of age, we became parents for the last time with our vivacious Isaiah.

Seven years into our heartbreaking situation, I had enough of a destructive marriage with Danny living in substance abuse. I finally got sick and tired of living with an alcoholic and gave an ultimatum. STOP your substance abuse or I will file for a separation. Before my ultimatum was given, I spent the first seven years of marriage in Christianity, demonstrating what a Proverbs 31 wife looked like to Danny. I served and loved him with all my heart as serving Jesus. I got up to make him dinner, as he arrived home by 2a.m. after partying. I learned to be self-controlled and not allow my emotions of anger and resentment to rule me. Danny saw what a character change I had undergone. He saw my devotion to God and to him. I asked for a change or I would now leave the marriage, Danny came home from spending an evening in jail and went straight to six am men's prayer group, it was there he gave his life to Christ and was instantly delivered of years of alcoholism and drug addictions! From that day to now, Danny was in church with us.

As I was feasting in the Word of God, the Word of God was tearing down my insecurities, my feelings of unworthiness, inferiority, insignificance, inadequacy, shame, guilt, self-loathing and building a God-Image within me. The Holy Spirit is a counselor, and he was my Post Abortion Counselor, as I forgave myself for the abortions. I realized the enemy of our soul always encourages us to sin and provides us with many reasons to sin and after we cooperate to do evil, he accuses us day and night with condemnation for doing what he encourages us to do! God on the other hand encourages us not to sin and after we disobey him, he is ever-present to forgive us and promises to remember our confessed sin no more!

My God Identity was being strengthened and empowered, my self-confidence was increasing, and all I could see was my ability to become a leader in the things of God was becoming clear. The Holy Spirit said to me, "My presence in you is mighty."

Feeding Paul, took two hours for breakfast, lunch, and dinner, he slept four short hours on the daily, so I was also up with Paul each night. Tony was six years old when Isaiah was born. I now knew what having twins was like, even though Paul was ten years old he was functioning as an infant, it was extremely difficult to feed them both. I was weary and agitated after ten years of caregiving. Nothing was working or changing in his life or improving in Paul's afflictions. I felt I must be doing something wrong, even though I was completely submerged in the word! I was confused and feeling fragmented because he was no better and things were about to take a devastating turn for the worst!

But I pressed on in the Word relentlessly, I was praying, fasting, serving, quoting scripture, living in purity and honesty, faithful and loyal to my husband and Christ, my intensity didn't wavier, I was a single-minded and I was determined to see Paul healed! I was as obedient to the Word of God as I knew how to be as the years went by with no improvements in his body!

I was Paul's only caregiver, and I was breaking down physically and mentally at this point, fatigue and exhaustion set in and I agonized over placing Paul, but I knew I couldn't go on like this. Later, we agreed to place Paul in a nearby house facility where competent people could help lift my load. After three months went by they suggested that a g-tube be placed in Paul's tummy so he could be properly nourished. We agreed to this very simple surgical procedure. All went well, and on the eve of his homecoming, I asked his nurse to place him on bed A because he couldn't be seen or heard on bed B. She assured me it would be done. On the morning of his discharge, the hospital called to tell me that Paul had a Cardiac Arrest and they resuscitated him. He was laid on his side and he kicked himself face down on the pillow while still in Bed B. He was never moved closer to the nurse station.

We waited for months to see the outcome of the Cardiac Arrest and loss of more oxygen to his brain. Paul was assigned to another facility an hour away from us because he could no longer breathe on his own, he now was put on life support, a ventilator. He could no longer drink or eat per mouth anymore because he could choke on water or food. His awareness of me dwindled and he no longer reacted to my voice. His body was deforming, contorting. He could only lie down on his back, he no longer could sit in a chair. His little body was now ridged and unyielding, the deformity was changing his soft limbs into hard paralyzed positions.

Every visit was a test of faith and trust, every visit stomped on my heart. I've never felt such excruciating grief, stabbings pains in my heart, viewing his deterioration for many years I just left numb, but I kept believing God for a resurrection.

Paul was in facility living now for 11 years, as Paul turned 21 he was transferred to a closer sub-acute facility for adults. At no time did anyone from the facility ever say we needed to decide to take Paul off life-support. So, I kept trusting when I couldn't trace God.

During this time in my spiritual life I was leading prayer groups as I moved in Tongues and Interpretation of Tongues, Prophecy and speaking at women's retreats, assisting in children's church and children's retreats, Teaching Women's Bible Classes and attending Bible College(s).

Our home front was strained at this time and the Holy Spirit showed me I was being dominated and verbally abused in marriage. I really couldn't detect this, as I thought Danny was just mad all the time, I was unaware that anger was a tactic and a red flag of verbal abuse. As I studied, I found we were a textbook case, he moved in several traits and I allowed it! After spending years now in the Word of God, I was ready to be used of the Holy Spirit to help bring awareness to my husband that he was being used of the enemy as a lethal weapon to destroy my self–esteem and self-worth, our enemy desires to mar and steal our identity so we are unable to reach destiny and destroy his kingdom! As I called out each tactic as he moved in it, he became aware and yielded to confrontation, correction, and consequences. It took time and it was a difficult turnaround, but we now have a mutually respectful relationship. The Holy Spirit's directive to him was "Support her in ministry." Danny is now my greatest cheerleader!

I was suffering from Panic Attacks since I was in my 20s, but the Holy Spirit told me three powerful truths that helped me gain victory. He said anxiety is thought related and thoughts control our lives, but I can control my thoughts, thirdly anxiety is a spirit of fear, and God didn't send me this spirit. I mediated the Peaceful Promises, capture and cast down evil imaginations, then replace with the Word. One day, I woke up and attacks were gone.

The Holy Spirit whispered to me your ministry has been tested, tried, and approved! My response was, "Lord, I don't have a ministry," it was years later he told me to start Morning Manna in my living room, so I began and after two years in my home, the Holy Spirit said now ask the women's leadership at the church if you can hold Morning Manna there. My ministry bloomed and blossomed there, they supported me with everything I needed for ministry to thrive, and I didn't have to pay a dime! It was during these years that I taught women how to Advance in Adversity, Progress In Pain, Move Forward Despite Hardships Isaiah 43:2

My ministry took off and Ekklesia Magazine featured us on the cover page several times, I was on Hope Radio Station many times, my first book was published, called Advance in Adversity, a Prophetic Devotional, at no cost! Speaking engagements were increasing, after my third Unifying Impact Unity Conference, a T.V. Broadcaster was in attendance and she asked me if she could interview me on her T.V.

program, this interview opened the door to the next series of promotions.

All the while visiting Paul and praying now, 'Your will be done!'

In July of 2017, I began my own T.V. Broadcast Show on the HSBN.TV Network, called Morning Manna. I received an Honorary Doctorate Degree and was ordained as an Apostle, a Co-Founder of the Christian Women's Word T.V. Network on CWWN. T.V. Network and Director of Evangelism at the Holy Spirit Broadcasting T.V. Network, we are bringing the Gospel to the Globe.

On Dec. 6th, 2017 God fulfilled his promise to me as our son Paul was healed! The care facility called us at 2a.m. and let us know he suffered a heart attack and passed. I had a decision to make, would I now resent God, rebel against God, or Rest in the decision God had made for us! What do you do with a God who can heal but says no, I am not healing your son on this side of heaven? I say, "Paul is well, so I'm well."

Paul fulfilled his purpose without speaking one word in 31 years, he came and kept me in the Secret Place long enough to establish a vibrant relationship with God, he came to teach me how to Advance in Adverse Seasons of life, he came to bless the lives of many through Morning Manna Ministries.

NAKITA "NIKKI" HERRERA: MY BODY...MY VALUE

Telling the truth about how I feel in my body, my stomach specifically, after having three children naturally and nine hernia surgeries. I'll start off by telling you how I got a hernia to begin with. It all started when I was 17 and pregnant. I was 105 pounds at first and went up to 160 pounds. After having my baby, pushing out the placenta, I felt something moving in my stomach. I was so scared, I looked down and I thought I had another baby in my stomach. The nurse said, "no sweetheart, it's a hernia." I said, "What is that? How did I get that?"

She said, "It's from straining, from pushing." She then says to me, you're going to need surgery soon. I'm like, "no, thanks." I wanted to breastfeed, so that's what I did for six weeks. I was in so much pain so I'm like *okay, I guess I have to get surgery.* I'm 17 years old, I'm petrified, and I had never had surgery. I'm a mom and I'm still a child. I was trying to be a mom, and I was already going through things. *17 years old remember that.* I'm glad to be a mom, but I tell you all, take your time. Anyways, I ended up getting surgery, and it was a small incision. Two-three staples and stitches right under my belly button. It hurt, but it wasn't a big deal, I healed. They told me I couldn't have another kid until I was 23. Umm yeah, I was hard-headed and didn't listen, and my hernia opened.

Ladies With Purpose

Fast forward, I had another kid. I'm 19 now, and my hernia opens up again and I had another surgery. Now, I'm healed, and NO, I didn't have any more kids for many years after, but I realized one day that I'd been in constant pain. I'm nauseated all the time. Some days I'm vomiting. My stomach started to get big. Now I'm freaking out because I know that my hernia was bigger. It went from a rubber ball bulge size to the size of a golf ball. This time it wasn't on my belly button or under it was above the belly button. They told me I needed surgery. Now, this is my third one. They had put something called a mesh in me and when they opened me up the saw that the mesh had balled up and my tissues had broken off. I had two kids with no epidural, but *this* pain was excruciating.

So now I have two kids and two surgeries. My stomach was already messed up because I had children, but now it was like, *ugh*. I didn't get lucky or blessed like other women. I didn't have that "snap back" as you all call it. The reason I wanted to talk about this, is because a lot of women don't talk about how they feel when it comes to their bodies after giving birth and having surgeries, such as a c-section. Whatever the case, it hurts, it scars. Giving life to another being is amazing, but it took a lot of my self-esteem.

People talked about me. People who said they loved me, *men in particular*. When we'd disagree or get in an argument, they'd say things like, "that's why you have stretch marks," or "that's why you have extra skin." So-called friends spoke down on my body. It may not be a big deal to some people, but it meant a lot to me. My stomach meant a lot to me. I used to work out every day. I would do sit-ups every morning. I took pride in it. I was athletic, I danced, drilled, cheered, *whatever*. It sucks that we must grow up in a world where people bash women for having stretch marks. We give life, and that in itself is everything. It took me all this time, from age seventeen, now age thirty-one, to even understand that and more importantly, accept that.

I believe with my whole heart that God was showing me how to love correctly. He was teaching me how to love from the inside and not for the outer appearance. The steps that I have been taking to overcome the many challenges and obstacles that have been flying at me are very simple. It's not easy but it is simple. First, acknowledge that you don't have it all together. *That is okay*. Stop letting people shame you for your trials and tribulations. It's what builds your character. Cry, let it out. I know I can speak for me when I say, I hate crying. I was always told that makes you weak. Growing up I held my tears back unless I got mad. Crying is good for your soul. *Don't you feel so free and empty when you let it out?* Overcoming many obstacles in my life, I know that my strength came from God. There were times I would go into a deep depression. People used to think I was so perfect, but really, I was broken inside. I am a survivor though.

When I relocated to California in 2011, I was a dancer. Yes, an exotic dancer. I felt as if it was my only way to survive. Newly single mom of two girls. Every day I went out to dance and every time I felt worse and worse. Slowly but surely, I felt like I was losing myself. So, I had been doing private parties on top of working at a club. One club I worked at our security guard was killed. He was so good to us, but he was shot multiple times with us all sitting upstairs. Coming outside and seeing his dead body slumped over, was the day I smoked my first cigarette. My now-deceased best friend Mariah Malvaeux and I were so spooked.

That was just the first incident where I felt God tugging on me, telling me to sit down. Of course, we always know best, so what happened, I do another private party, and a guy walks straight in the doors and started shooting. All I see are sparks coming toward me. My boo-thang was shot in his arm. I'm panicking holding my friend on the ground as blood is leaking. This was the day I woke and said *you know what God, I'm done. I don't want to die. I love my kids I just want to be better for them.* I kid you not, 2013 I got saved and I quit smoking, drinking, and dancing. When I tell you, God loves me, He does. I shouldn't be here, but He gave me a purpose that I plan to fulfill. Ladies, life may seem like it's throwing so much at you at one time, but just know God has a plan for everything. His ways are bigger

171

than our ways. Live your life for you. Live, love, laugh. God wants us to go out and preach His message – the kingdom message. Stay prayed up and in your word, everything else will follow.

I've never known what my purpose was in life, but I always knew when I came in contact with people, I was supposed to leave an everlasting impression on them. In life, that's all we can do. Sometimes you're not going to understand why this person did this, or this person did that...or why this person left you. Or this person betrayed you. Or just left out your life with no explanation. All you can do is tell yourself, *I must have achieved my purpose with them, and my time in their life is up and I'm off to the next person to bless with everything you offer as a person.* This goes for friendships and relationships.

I thank everyone who is still in my life.
And I thank everyone who is gone.
God bless.

CHRISTINE NORDMARK: FINAL TESTAMONY

I was young and made a lot of bad choices. I don't know if it was because I felt abandoned as a little girl by my dad, or if I had so much self-hatred that I felt like I deserved to live in total misery.

I ended up in a horrible relationship that was very abusive at a very young age. I found myself pregnant, and he told me that I was going to have an abortion. He already had a child and didn't want another one. I didn't understand. I thought a baby would make things better. He took me down to get an abortion against my will. He warned me that if I didn't have the abortion, he would abort the baby for me. So, out of fear, I complied. When I went into the clinic, they lied to me and told me that it was nothing but a piece of flesh. Now before that baby would've been born, I got pregnant again. I told him that abortion is not birth control, but he didn't care. This time I had a plan for when he took me down to the abortion clinic against my will. I asked the nurse if I could talk to the doctor beforehand so I could tell him to just keep me in the back so my boyfriend would think I went through with the abortion. She said, "Sure, honey. Let me just get your IV going, and I'll get the doctor for you." I woke up with an empty womb. I felt betrayed and broken. Once you go into an abortion clinic, you do not leave with a baby inside of you. The blood of my child is on her hands! Before that baby would've been born, it happened again. This time I had told him, no...but he had been drinking and didn't listen. I knew I would end up pregnant, and I was devastated. I literally had to escape from him. His mom threatened to beat me up, and I knew I had to move away to save my baby. A couple of days later, I started bleeding. I went to the hospital, and the doctor told me I was having a spontaneous abortion. I prayed to God to save this child. I begged Him to please let this one live! Three days later, I went back to the hospital, and they told me that my pregnancy hormones were normal. God answered my prayers! I promised Him I would dedicate this child to Him all the days of its life! I knew I was going to have to do this on my own. My boyfriend threatened me and told me he didn't want his name on the birth certificate because he didn't want to have to take financial responsibility for this child. He told me to say that I got drunk at a party and I didn't remember who the father was. Halfway through the pregnancy, I started getting letters from him while he was in jail. He manipulated me and told me he had changed, had become a Christian, and he wanted to reconcile. I was very hopeful, so I gave him another chance. During the time he was in jail, I had to get on welfare for the baby. Nine months after our son was born, we went to Laughlin and got married at a little chapel. I cried during the ceremony, knowing in my heart that I was making a mistake. I thought getting married would make things better, but I found out quickly how very wrong I was. After we got married, the abuse got worse.

He told me not to get off welfare because we needed the support. Now I was his possession, so the physical, verbal, and emotional abuse kept getting more frequent. Every time I would try to leave, he would either strangle me, run me off the road, or tell me he would bury me in the backyard. Several years went by, and things weren't getting better. In fact, he was cheating and starting to get abusive in front of the children. It was one thing for him to hurt me behind closed doors, but when he started doing it in front of the children...I couldn't take it anymore. He told me that if I left him, he would turn me in for welfare fraud. I felt betrayed and was blackmailed into staying with him as long as I did because of the children. He threatens to take my stepdaughter away from me if I leave him. I had no idea that he had this blackmail planned all along.

This wasn't the first time he had done that to a woman who was pregnant with his child. His daughter also had a birth certificate which said, "father unknown." I found out he had many other babies aborted previously. During the time he was threatening me not to leave, he had gotten another woman pregnant. I told him that he made his bed, and he needed to lay in it. This was finally my way out. After he left, I bought a gun to protect myself because there would be times I would come home, and he would be sitting on the stairs just waiting for me. I was afraid that he would come and kill me in the middle of the night while I was sleeping. Sure enough, my worst fear came true.

The neighbors started telling me that there was an investigator at their door asking about us. I was scared and didn't know what to do. I started calling attorneys and shared my story with them. They told me that anything over $500 was considered a felony for welfare fraud, and I could go to prison for two years. The attorneys also told me that domestic violence was not considered a valid excuse for the fraud. I just remember being in a very dark place feeling like there was no hope, no light at the end of the tunnel. I know the devil was lying to me. I had a gun, and I felt like it was my only way out. I just couldn't imagine this man blackmailing me and having me put in prison for something he planned and taking my son away...while getting away with it! I called up the secretary at the attorney's office and asked her to please meet me, so I could give her the gun, so I wouldn't use it until the investigation was over. She met with me and locked the gun in their safe. I remember not being able to eat or sleep for days. I was in so much fear and completely tormented in my mind with the thought of going to prison and losing my son to him.

My "Jesus freak" aunt called me one night and told me that the Lord wanted me to read **Isaiah 26:3-4**. I asked her how the Lord told her that and she just said that while she was praying the Lord prompted her to tell me that I needed to read the scripture verses.

So, she called me to tell me. I wrote the verses down on a piece of paper and forgot about them for a couple of days. Finally, when I couldn't take it anymore, I found a Bible and opened it up. To my surprise, it opened up exactly at **Isaiah 26:3-4**. I looked up and said, "okay, Lord, I think You're trying to tell me something."

I read aloud the scripture that said, **"you will keep him in perfect peace whose mind is stayed on you because he trusts in you, trust in the Lord forever, for He is the eternal rock."** I felt warm oil pour over me from the top of my head to the bottom of my feet and I instantly had complete and total peace.

Three days later, I went to visit my Grammy on my dad's side. She said, "Tina, the Lord wanted me to give this to you," and handed me a laminated card that had the scripture **Isaiah 26:3-4** on it. I couldn't believe it! That's when I saw the Lord's hands reach down from heaven and use my aunt and my grandmother to show me that He was real and that He was with me! I prayed and completely gave my life over to Him and asked Him to defend me during the investigation. My attorney and I went to the investigator and for hours I told him everything that had happened over the past several years. When we left the room, the investigator came out and told my attorney that he would be going down to the district attorney's office in the morning and letting him know that he would not be pressing charges against me. The Lord defended me!

That was just the beginning of my journey of faith. We ended up in a vicious divorce and child custody battle for the next ten years that tested and tried my faith and drew me closer to Jesus Christ! Since then, God has worked everything out in such miraculous ways!

My ex passed away suddenly of a heart attack at 41 years old after I had led him to the Lord. I started praying for him two years before he died and the Lord gave me a love that could only come from Jesus Christ. I completely forgave him for everything. The word of God says that He will not forgive us if we don't know forgive others.

The Lord brought me the most wonderful husband from over 2,000 miles away that I could've ever dreamt for. God is so faithful and He restored everything that the locusts had eaten in my life. He blessed us with two beautiful daughters. God has been gracious every day of my life! He has all of us on a journey and will use what seems to be very painful events to bring us into a very precious and close relationship with our Father in heaven! He wants an intimate relationship with each one of His children. He loves our oceans and seas more than we could ever imagine! When you give your life to Jesus, He will help you to fulfill the destiny, purpose, and plan that God wrote for your life! And on that day after you've finished your race you will hear, "Well done, my good and faithful servant, enter into My Kingdom that was prepared for you from the foundations of the world!"

"Not all of us can do great things. But we can do small things with great love."

YOLANDA BANKS: DEALING WITH CONFLICT

I was asked by my friend and sister in Christ to be a part of her project she and her husband are working on. I am thankful she thought about me. I am delighted, a little scared but ecstatic about the opportunity before me. I hope more than anything whoever reads this piece of work finds it helpful, insightful, and inspiring. May it be helpful in your daily life, but most of all help you build more resistance to handle conflict.

This pandemic (Coronavirus) has taught me to appreciate life a lot more and time really waits for no one. *Be Blessed.*

KNOW THYSELF (CHANGING WORLD)

This year has been very interesting and life-changing on many levels. The world changed in March 2020, and it will never be the same as it once was. The Coronavirus and George Floyd's death has brought on a string of events that the world as a whole will never forget.

The police brutality of Afro-American people and the senseless killings by the hands of the people who are paid to "protect and serve" and make the environment unsafe for us all. The police decided that black men and women's lives were for taking and put in a place of a horrible tactic to pat each other on the back and say, "good job we got another." How horrible is it to think Afro-American people can be gunned down in front of everyone, strangled to death in broad daylight, and have a police officer put his knee on the back of a man's neck and kill him with no remorse.

I have read books about slavery and the treatment my people endured. But in a changing world, the mistreatment of Afro-American men and women is ongoing and consistent in every way possible. The world reacted to George Floyd's death because he was another victim who suffered and died in the hands of the police. Thank God for cameras because the world had to see this man pleading for his life and die. The world responded and the protest began. People of every color were wanting to see the change in the process, procedures, literature, and the way of the world. There is conflict all around and the breaking point broke and it erupted. Small changes are being made in the Black Lives Movement but everyone is wanting change, accountability held, and justice for all. So you say, how does this fit in with, "Know Thyself." Here are a couple of scripture quotes about knowing yourself:

1 Corinthians 11:28-29 KJV

But let a man examine himself, and so let him eat of (that) bread, and drink of (that) cup. For he that eateth and drinketh unworthily, eateth and drinketh damnation to himself, not discerning the Lord's body.

2 Corinthians 13:5 KJV

Examine yourselves, whether ye be in the faith; prove your own selves. Know ye, not your own selves, how that Jesus Christ is in you, except ye be reprobates?

The only way to know thyself is to examine yourself. Self examination should be part of your well-being. Yes, it can be frightening but a must in order for you to feel secure and confident within yourself. When you examine yourself, you don't let trigger words control you. You are not enraged about every little thing but the right things. You hold your composer and answer when you have gained better insight into the situation. This is a constant drill practice for me. I do not get excited about what everyone says, I started really watching what I do and my reactions to certain circumstances. I thought I knew myself pretty well. But I started to dig deeper and I realized that there was some work to be done if I wanted to see a change. I have not stopped the practice; I still check myself daily. No one is perfect but if you are in conflict with oneself, that may be where the problem of handling conflict begins. Getting to know yourself requires loneliness, research, moments with God, and learning that peace is more important. I began this journey several years ago and I am glad I did. It has helped me with my feelings (I feel everything), new discoveries, and paying attention to areas I did not give much attention to.

Knowing thyself is not an easy journey you have to be real with yourself. You have to want to change and ask for help while you change. How do you know thyself? Here are a couple of avenues I took but I am sure there are more depending on the type of conflicts you incur. If you believe in God, start there by reading your bible. Make it a part of your daily regimen. When I looked back on some of the conflicts I was dissatisfied by the way I handled some of them. My motto was when I get tired of you. If I said something wrong to you, oh well, and kept it rolling. See, I do not like to be around or tolerate people and their mess. There was one situation that made me change my mind. I lashed out and now they know how I feel. Problem solved and I moved on and you will not be spoken to, acknowledged, or participate with me on anything, bye Felicia. But I got a call and we were speaking about the way we handle situations. Remember, I wanted to change so I had to go back and apologize for some of the things I said. Sometimes I did not understand why some conflicts were even conflicts, but that did not matter I wanted to change the way I dealt with conflicts and the outcome of them. I kept at it and pressed to get a resolution about the way I handle conflicts going forward. I say this, but please remember every situation is different and you might not get it right the first time but keep going, the benefits are rewarding for you and others. You learn to be a more thoughtful person because words can hurt.

MEDITATION

I started meditating about four years ago. I sit still and let my mind, body settle into a state of ease, no resistance of letting go. I do deep breathing practices and stretching to allow my body to release the tension and stress. There are different forms of meditation you can use. I currently use several different ones.

PRAYING

I find praying helps me stay present and grounded. This builds your relationship with God. No one can take your prayer life away from you. This is an individual process, and it does not depend on anyone but you. If you believe in the Father, he needs to hear from you. How do you expect God to help you through some of the difficult times we face?

BUILD CONFIDENCE

Learning about yourself in and out is so life-changing and joyous. It is the best thing you can do for you. Read books about how our people struggled and who we are in the Bible. Go and read some of the quotes from our black leaders, and see which ones resonate with you. Pick up Marcus Garvey, Malcom X, and others and read what these men before us learned and wanted to implement. Building up your confidence and creating room for change. Get fit and eat healthily. Make it a priority and set some goals. Live your best life what is going on. My people will shine again.

THYSELF

Allow yourself to get upset without blaming someone else. Make yourself accountable to yourself. Do not wait for someone to call you to make you happy. Call yourself and tell yourself daily affirmations and quotes to build and feed the inside. Put in the work and be honest. Get in some You and You time. Pamper the outside of the body. Do not use harsh products on it, make sure it soft and smooth to your touch. Prepare for bed at night and make it a pleasant atmosphere to be in. Check the inside and outside they go hand and hand. Self-examinations/knowing thyself are critical to your growth. It is for you and only you. The road may be bumpy, not sure how it is going to work out, and want to stop. Do not stop or give up but knowing you are working on something great and making the necessary changes to work on, changes that build steps to feeling better and knowing thyself.

THE LIFE TRAJECTORY OF
AUDREY MARIE BROUSSARD-HOLMES

Begins in the small sector of the county of Los Angeles, called WATTS, California where she was born and raised. Born to a two-parent household, Audrey and her older brother would later be joined by three other brothers and sisters. Growing up in a household of eight children ensured that money would always be tight with many days of limited provisions as experienced by other families that resided in the WATTS community.

Audrey was raised in a Christian home with her father being ordained has a Pentecostal pastor of a small store-front church. This factor would later prove to play a pivotal role in her life trajectory.

Growing up in WATTS in what was referred to as the "turbulent 60s", Audrey experienced the terror and community instability caused by the WATTS riots of 1965. That experience highlighted by the national guard creating a command post in her backyard would mark her resilience for years to come.

Attending Jordan High School in WATTS, Audrey excelled scholastically and acquiring leadership skill sets, volunteering in her community learning at an early age the importance of using her skills and abilities to enhance and help to rebuild her community.

Ladies With Purpose

One of the groups that Audrey would participate in was the California Scholarship Federation. It was through her involvement in this organization that the desire to attend a college or university was born. Here she as able to aspire to an ambitious life beyond the confines of the improvised WATTS community. It was her scholastic aptitude and community volunteerism that afforded her the opportunity to apply and be accepted into one of the premier universities in the country, The University of Southern California. Audrey was selected to receive a four-year scholarship considered as a "full-ride" to attend USC complete with the monetary coverage to live on campus in the dormitory. She went on to graduate within four years, attaining a Bachelor of Science Degree in Education.

Upon graduating from USC, Audrey began her professional career with Los Angeles Unified School District (LAUSD) as an elementary school teacher. She taught in the South-Central Watts community as a way of giving back and helping the young children still impacted by the systemic failures that negatively impacted the residents of her community: economic, housing, educational, and judicial systems.

Audrey would later leave the LAUSD system and embark on a journey that would expose her to other systems seeking to address the deficiencies that existed in the South Central/WATTS community. Her initial experience was with the Los Angeles Job Corps Center. There she was introduced to skillsets needed to assist the youth who had dropped out of high school, faced youth incarceration, and/or were connected to the foster-care system. The initial position as an Exit World of Work Instructor. She would be introduced to the field of employment training and career development. This position would also afford her the opportunity to participate in different learning groups designed to equip the staff in acquiring access to the resources needed by "youth-at-risk."

At that point in her professional career, Audrey became aware of her purpose. This clarity was even more clearly identified during her professional service to the City of Compton, as a Senior Employment Training Specialist within the Department of

Ladies With Purpose

Employment Training Services. It was during her tenure with the City of Compton that Audrey returned to college (CSULB), to obtain a post-graduate Master of Public Administration (MPA) Degree with a Certificate in Grant Management. MPA degree in hand, and armed with the Certificate in Grants management, she immediately began her work with designing programs to positively impact the lives of underserved populations, beginning with the position of Program Manager with LA County Office of Education and later with the LA County Community Development Commission. This work focused on developing programs, activities, services, and resources designed to enhance the life trajectory of individuals facing multiple barriers to selected sufficiency.

This work leads to Audrey accepting a management position with the United Auto Workers-Labor Employment Training Corporation (UAW-LETC), promoting the management ladder to the level of Chief Operating Officer (COO). During her tenure, she was responsible for the development of numerous programs and resources designed to mitigate the negative impacts of systemic racism and societal neglect and improvised impacts.

Audrey's professional career was further enhanced by engaging programs, funding, and resources designed to positively impact the lives of individuals experiencing homelessness, formerly incarcerated/gang members, veterans, and those seeking career pathway development due to the elimination of certain labor market-driven industries. One of such assignment as the Director of Workforce Development with Homeboy Industries, a nationally recognized reentry and gang intervention program that utilizes Social Enterprises to create a career pathway learning environment. She has held the operational titles of Senior Manager, Director, Area Administrator, Vice President, and Chief Operating Officer.

She is currently a consultant serving in various grant, local, state, and federally funded programs and projects. As a Believer in the Lordship of Jesus Christ, Audrey is fully aware of God's Sovereign Purpose in her chose profession. She realizes on the premise found in **Roman 8 vs. 28: Knowing that she is called according to HIS purpose.**

SHELLIE A. HUNT: NOT THE VICTIM… BUT A VISIONARY

There have been so many things in my life that could have broken my spirit. Once, I was asked if I were to write a book about my life story, what title I would give my story. I answered, "unbroken." There are many things that have happened in my life that could have easily made me distrusting, bitter, and emotionally disengaged. We can all find excuses if we look at life as if we are a victim. Our lives are not defined only by what has happened to us. Instead, life is defined by our ability to move through the challenges and progress as an individual.

Look at how diamonds are made. How does a dusty rock turn into a brilliant and clear gem? A diamond only becomes a diamond by being subjected to intense heat and intense pressure. During my life, I faced poverty, bone-crushing car accidents, dyslexia, multiple rapes and sexual assaults, a brutal home invasion, years of domestic violence, issues of self-perfection, divorce, and oh, let's not forget buying other people's baggage and making excuses for those around me to be negative. I have come to realize, that any one of these circumstances could have halted my personal, professional, and social growth. Had I acted from a victim mentality, I could have allowed any one of these circumstances to be an out or a chicken exit. Being a

185

single mom from the very beginning of my pregnancy, I could have decided not to have a career. During my first few years as a mom, I could have bought a story that I, a single mother, could not have both a family and a successful career. Now, I share this not to diminish the feelings of those affected by circumstances outside of their control. During the most difficult times in my life, I definitely wondered if I was going to make it through, but I did, once I took control of my emotions about the situations. From each of my experiences, I have repeatedly come to realize that nothing becomes great without great resistance!

When I was asked how I got through each of these events with such perseverance, I realized that my ability to move forward from each of these circumstances was correlated to my ability to see the blessings within the struggle. My ability to enact strength, compassion, leadership, and confidence within every obstacle I overcame helped me to emerge from the pressure better than before. At times, I would ask myself *why is this happening to me,* not knowing that it was not the event, but my reaction to the events in my life that would leave a lasting impression upon myself and my self-worth.

It's important to be aware that you can buy other people's baggage and adopt it as your own story. You are not your story! I see many that have lived life hiding in the stories of the past. One such example is we all know a woman that walks around bitter from divorce and untrusting to the point that it leaves a lasting impact on every future relationship that she enters into. I remember at the end of my marriage I had a choice to make about how I wished to emotionally leave a marriage in which my partner was dishonest. Rather than taking the opinion that all men can't be trusted due to the infidelity of my ex, I decided that marriage was good, but that I had found the wrong guy. Had I blamed all men that would have been baggage that I carried forward? As I moved on, I found out that I had to be very vigilant in my thought processes and in my choices. When we take the time to achieve self-awareness during our most difficult circumstances we can emerge from these events as diamonds, having survived the pressure to shine brighter than ever before.

The next time you face adversity, and you will remember YOU are here to be a diamond, walking in feminine grace and all is just refining with blessings bestowed so we may be strong leading us to our life of service and leading with purpose.

CEU / Founder of Women of global change

CONCLUSION

Hello My Dear,

Get inspired to channel your inner warrior princess with these awesome life stories from women for women. You are strong, confident, and courageous, and these powerful testimonies will serve as your perfect reminder of just that!

Women provide the foundation of power, grace, wisdom, justice, creativity, and hope.

Women are known to have a great sense of intuition, patience, emotional focus, compassion, and networking ability. The list of female strengths *are* endless.

Loss can either consume us or push us into a new direction. Having experienced the loss of people in my life, I agree we carry the loss with us, and over time we get through the grief. Keep sharing your story and touching others' lives in a positive way. Keep going, you're a strong woman.

ABOUT THE AUTHOR

There are some who stay silent and bear, then there are those who speak up and fight. Throughout history, the world has witnessed many great women of strength who managed to tap into their everyday power to leave an indelible mark on society. Reading words of wisdom from such amazing women can inspire you to become a strong woman yourself, who approaches life with confidence. These "women of steel," have inspired many to be brave and never let anyone or anything stop them from being the best version of themself. Salute to their undying spirit!

Yolanda Yvette Everett is an astounding mentor and preacher speaker. Her passion is to *empower, encourage, excite, and ignite* young ladies to pursue who they are and their career dreams. She is the founder and CEO of Ladies with Purpose Foundation, a non-profit organization whose vision is "To Enhance the Quality of Life for Young Ladies." Yolanda graduated from California State University, Los Angeles, with a double BA Degree in Psychology and Criminology. She furthered her education and received her MA Degree in Criminology with an emphasis on Statistical Criminal Behavior. Yolanda attended Los Angeles School of Ministry and certification and license in Christian Counselor and Pastoral Care.

Mrs. Everett accepted the call to ministry in 1987 and was installed as Associate Pastor in 2000. Pastor Yolanda was married on February 13, 2016, to her soul mate Jamil "Honey" Everett. This dynamic duo are authors of several books, one being *From Brokenness to Wholeness*, by which they have organized a ministry with the same name. Pastor Yolanda and Minister Jamil have six children jointly and 13 grandchildren. Their prayer is that "above all things that you may prosper and be in health, even as your soul prospers."

Ladies With Purpose
CEO / President
Yolanda Y. Everett., BA., MA

In loving memory

Deborah Pattynama

Mother JoAnn Johnson

Founded in 1994, Ladies with Purpose, hereafter noted as LWP. The main service area of this organization is Riverside County, however, San Bernardino County, as well as Orange and Los Angeles Counties' residence are welcome to become participants. Our mission is to "improve the lives of those young ladies who have been down-trodden and have issues with low self-esteem and no directives or guidance in life, through comprehensive support services, such as counseling and mentoring, and to assist them through education and training how to be self-sufficient young women."

The purpose of this organization is to assist in the personal, one on one, self-esteem building, and empowerment of young ladies. This ministry will attend fashion shows, receive makeovers, and attend beauty consulting training to assist them in how to dress and how not to dress. They will also receive clarification on the various fads of dressings and their awful negative connotation. The other purpose of this ministry is to minister to those young ladies that have been abused and misused, and minister healing to their souls. I have come across, within the last 25 years, young ladies that have been outcasts, abused, and misused by not only man but society as well. God has given me the desire, the dream the ministry of reconciliation, to help these young ladies. All of them are single parents who seem to have lost both hope and directions. It is my desire through the leading and wisdom and knowledge of the Holy Spirit to shed light, understanding, and bring hope back to these ladies. It is my desire, as it is the desire of the Lord God for them to be self-sufficient young mothers, taking care of their children and loving God, as their priority in their lives until God bless them with a man after His own heart. Eventually, hopes are to open this up to young men as well. The overall objective is to make this group an Inland Empire based organization. Other topics such as dating and sex, along with other crucial topics will be discussed.

Ladies with Purpose Staff and Board can be reached at yladywpurpose@yahoo.com

www.ingramcontent.com/pod-product-compliance
Lightning Source LLC
Chambersburg PA
CBHW050128030726
47505CB00007B/2083